My Journey With Jesus and Jo

Richard G. Marshall

and

Poems by Jo

Melba J. Marshall

with comments by Richard G. Marshall

Cover art and editing by Jenifer E. Grover

Brushpanther Press

Copyright © 2008 by Richard G. Marshall

All rights reserved. No part of this book may be reproduced in any form by any means without express written permission from the author, except by a reviewer who may quote brief passages in a review.

Brushpanther Press
2813 Pinehurst Lane, Huntington, WV 25704

Paperback first edition.

Author's note: This is an autobiographical and biographical work. To the best of the author's knowledge all dates, places, and names of people are correct.

Bible quotations are from the King James Version (*KJV*) or the Revised Standard Version (*RSV*).

Library of Congress Control Number: 2008936671

ISBN 978-0-615-25039-7

Front cover photo by Bernice Golden (1957).
Back cover photos, clockwise L-R: Melba J. Marshall (1962), Margaret Kapanka (1957), Richard G. Marshall (1970), John Nicely (1982), Richard G. Marshall (1957), Michael Pawlowicz (1978), Robert B. Green (1981). Lower photo by Jenifer E. Grover (2008).

Printed in the United States of America

*To the Honor and Glory of God
in Loving Memory of
Melba Josephine Marshall
and our sons
Gerald Keith, Kenneth Stuart and Ian Douglas*

My Journey With Jesus and Jo

Take delight in the Lord and He will give you the desires of your heart.   Psalm 37:4, RSV

Richard G. Marshall

Table of Contents

Foreword	9
1 - The Reckoning	11
2 - The Beginning of Recovery	15
3 - A Spiritual Find	19
4 - Rebuilding Life	21
5 - The Path Gets Rough	25
6 - Our Union	27
7 - We Begin a Family	33
8 - The Horizon Broadens	37
9 - We Become Southerners	41
10 - Tragedy Strikes Again	47
11 - Picking up the Pieces	49
12 - Changes	51
13 - Questions (and Answers)	55
14 - Born Again	59
15 - The Wind Blows Where it Will	61
16 - The Call	65
17 - Living Waters	67
18 - New Vistas	69
19 - The Call Takes Shape	79
20 - Deep in the Heart of Texas	83
21 - Church Ministry Begins	91
22 - Family Changes	93
23 - Life at St. Andrew's	97
24 - Back Into Space	101
25 - Re-entry	105
26 - Florida Re-visited	107
27 - Control Issues	109
28 - Bane and Blessing	113
29 - Leaving Huntsville	117
30 - Beginnings in Florida	121
31 - Settling In	125
32 - Our World is Shattered	131
33 - The Healing Road	133
34 - The End of Our World	139
Afterword	141

Foreword

Many times my conversations with other people have become counseling or witnessing sessions. I sometimes draw upon my own experiences to illustrate a point or a concept. On several occasions people have told me, "You ought to write a book about your experiences."

While talking with a neighbor five days before Christmas of 2006, I stopped in the middle of our conversation and said, "Here I am telling my story again." The neighbor replied, "That is what you need to do." Then it seemed like I heard the Lord telling me, "This is want I want you to do – tell your story." On Christmas Day I started writing this book..

To me, this is the simple story of a somewhat simple man who made (and still makes) many mistakes in his life, but I found redemption, purpose, and direction in Our Lord Jesus Christ, and found true love on this earth with my wife, Melba Josephine. The story begins at that point in my life when I realized my need for redemption. As I looked back over my life in telling this story, I could see that there was always an unseen hand patiently guiding, often giving, sometimes restraining, but never compromising my free will. As I became more open to the Lord, I found myself more often in what I believed was direct communication with Him.

These imperfect words are written in tribute to a most perfect God, and as a memorial to the wonderful woman who shared her life with me for more than fifty years, who set aside her goal to become a concert pianist and became a wife and mother, who gave up her career in gospel music and radio to support my preparation for ministry. Jo's life was a life of love: Love of God, love of me, love of Jenifer, love of family, love of friends, love of animals, love of the arts, love of life itself. Even during times of anger, her anger was borne out of love.

It is my hope that these words will inspire, encourage, help, or comfort others on their journey.

I am deeply grateful to our daughter, Jenifer Elaine Grover, for the encouragement and help she has given me, and for her untiring effort in getting this story ready for publication. My sincere thanks to Fr. David Allert for reviewing the first draft of this book and giving me his comments.

                                        The Rev. Richard G. Marshall
                                        St. Augustine, Florida
                                        May 16, 2008

1 – The Reckoning

"If I die tonight, I'll go to Hell!" This was the judgment I passed upon myself.

It was the night after Christmas, 1953. I had left my wife, Mona, and Richard Brian, our seven-year-old son, at home while I went to see a movie by myself. After the show I had a hamburger and malted milk, and then went home. It was near midnight. I was sitting alone in the living room when my chest started pounding like a massive heartbeat. I didn't know what was happening and an immense feeling of fear came over me.

Overwhelmed with panic, I started throwing up violently. I remember focusing on the self-winding watch I was wearing, believing I would go on living as long as it kept running. Suddenly the pounding stopped. I was sure my heart had quit, that I was going to die, and judged myself deserving of nothing other than eternal damnation. I felt then and there that for years I had been living the wrong kind of life and that I had to get right with God.

Mona got out of bed and called our doctor. It was one o'clock in the morning, but he insisted on seeing me right away. After we got to his office he examined me thoroughly. The crisis was over, but recovery would not be easy. I had experienced a physical breakdown somewhat akin to a nervous breakdown. My stomach would not tolerate anything but weak black tea or ice water. My thyroid had quit functioning, my blood pressure was dangerously low, and I was iron deficient. Three years of hard, fast living had finally taken its toll.

I was twenty-five years old, in my fourth year of taking twelve hours a week of engineering courses at Lawrence Institute of Technology while working full-time as the manager of seven people in an accounting office.

I was a high school dropout at fifteen and a half, but went back to finish high school five years later. I wanted to go to public day school, but could not get an afternoon or night shift job, so I enrolled in night school. Ten months later I lost my job and was not able to get another day job. However, I did get a night shift job on an assembly line at Chrysler, which then made day school possible. I enrolled at Lincoln High School in Ferndale, Michigan, and graduated in 1950 with A's and a scholarship to Lawrence Tech. I felt most fortunate that I was able to finish in the public school system and receive full accreditation for my education, as well as a college scholarship.

After high school I went to work in the stock accounting office at Long Manufacturing, a company that made automotive radiators and clutches. I also started college in night school. In the summer of 1953 I was promoted to office manager. I had a near "A" average in college and was successful with everything I tried.

School and work were not enough. I had been president of my fraternity, Kappa Phi Sigma, was president of the Student Council, attended every social event, and bar hopped every Friday night after school. My life was one of hard work, hard play, and hard drinking. Any morality I possessed was undoubtedly a product of early religious upbringing, an innate idealism, and probably a lack of acceptable opportunity (I thank God for that). I had a high degree of ambivalence, however, and felt like I wanted to have an outside love affair, as so many of my peers were doing.

But now the vehicle had broken down. I managed to keep working, but dropped all but the five easiest hours of school. My mother, Hazel, strenuously objected to our doctor's allowing me to go back to work and school after just a few days of bed rest, but he told her, "Right now it is important that we keep his mind occupied. Don't worry, his body will not allow him to damage it any further." He was right; I could only do so much without becoming completely fatigued.

Ten days after the onslaught I was allowed my first solid food, a baked potato with nothing on it. It was the best meal I ever ate. The doctor prescribed thyroxin and a regimen of weekly iron shots. Along the way I developed a serious sinus infection, and went to Florida with my mother and young Richard to recover. When we returned, it was too late for me to enroll in the spring semester. This forced me to reluctantly take time off, but this was time that I badly needed for healing.

Not forgotten was the resolution to get my spiritual life in order; I did not like the threat of Hell I had experienced.

I had quit going to church after Mona and I were married; I just didn't feel the need of it. I had grown up in the Presbyterian Church and tried going back there, then I tried the Lutheran Church, and finally settled somewhat on my parents' Methodist church, but none of these felt like the place I needed to be. I resisted going to the Episcopal Church, because that was Mona's church. For some reason that seemed to be a concession to her I did not want to make. I didn't try any of the evangelical churches, because there were none close by, I had no familiarity with them, and I didn't know anyone who could introduce me to one.

2 – The Beginning of Recovery

By late spring of 1954 my health was improving. I wanted to spread my wings and enjoy the new ivory Ford convertible I had bought the previous fall. Ray, a young man who worked in our purchasing department and frequently visited our office, and I put together a swimming party at Cass Lake State Park.

Ray invited Dolores and Jo, the two youngest girls who worked for me, and they accepted. Off we went on June 11th, with shrimp dinners, beer for us, and Cokes for the girls. Ray paired off with Dolores, and I did with Jo; everything was above board, it was just a fun outing.

Jo was something else. It was June of '53 when Miss Melba Josephine Golden started work in the stock accounting office. I was not yet the manager; that came a month or so later. She was small, had natural blond hair, and was fresh out of high school. She walked in wearing a blue tweed suit, harlequin glasses, and white bobby sox over stockings. I thought she was the prettiest girl I had ever seen, and wished that I could even dare think of having someone like her to love. I sure did enjoy seeing her every day at work.

The end of each year brought the task of closing that year's books, and that always meant working Saturdays. Jo did not have a way of getting to work on Saturday, so I drove her to work and back home. During these times we got to know each other pretty well. The first time I picked her up I thought of her as a teenybopper who would really moan when I turned on CBN, the Canadian station that played classical music. Turned out that CBN was her favourite station, and that she had studied classical piano and voice. She loved all music; it was her life.

I knew that Jo was dating a friend from her church, but I didn't know how serious it was. I did not entertain any ideas that there could ever be anything between us. It just seemed too remote, too impossible.

After we left the state park, I drove Dolores home, took Ray to his car, then drove Jo home. I let her out of the car and we just stood there looking at each other. Impulsively I said, "Jo, I love you!"

She replied, "I love you too."

We kissed, and both felt like we had been handed hot burning coals.

A dinner date followed a week later at The Ponchartrain Cellar, a

French restaurant in downtown Detroit. Jo was so shy and nervous that she could only eat a few bites of her wild duckling dinner. A week later we saw an adventure movie. I had persuaded Jo that my marriage was a shambles. The question arose, "Where do we go from here?" An affair with someone like Jo was out of the question. I loved her too much for that. Yet, I was not free to marry.

My life with Mona was miserable. She was not a good homemaker and lacked good personal habits. When she wasn't working, neighbors complained about her visiting and keeping them from their work. Mona was an adept businesswoman and a good person, but she just didn't seem to know how to be a responsible wife or mother.

July 4th came on a Sunday, and I was in turmoil about what to do. I had found love, was trying to get godly order in my life, and my conscience had me tied in knots. I went to the minister of our Methodist church the next day and confessed my situation to him. He prayed for me, but did not offer any kind of counsel. That weekend I tried to reconcile with Mona.

The next day I told Jo I could not go on seeing her, that I had to try to patch up my marriage. She took it quietly, was obviously hurt, and was very cool toward me (understandably so). About a week later, Jo came to my desk and said, "I cannot stay mad at you." I told her that I was miserable with the decision I had made and miserable without her. We started seeing each other again. Thus began an exhilarating time of going to operas and ballets at the Masonic Auditorium, art movies at the Krim Theatre, and dinners at the wonderful restaurants that Detroit offered. Jo was a terrific dresser and I was most proud to be seen with her.

Meanwhile, Jo's mother, Bernice, became aware of our dating, and I knew I would have to meet with her and take whatever was coming. I went into their living room with Jo. Bernice was just sitting there. Jo's father, Neil, was not there and I was much relieved. I was more than a little anxious about facing one angry parent, much less two. Her mother was serious, but gentle and calm. I told her that I loved Jo and did not want to hurt her in any way. She said she trusted Jo and would trust me also. What a wonderful, loving woman – no anger, no lecturing, just concern, and confidence in the way she had raised her daughter. I knew then that decisions had to be made, and made soon.

I felt a real need to get away and clear my head. I persuaded my uncle, Harold Cook, to go with me on a wilderness canoe trip to

Chapleau, Ontario. We went in August and it was quite an adventure. We got a canoe, tent, and supplies in Chapleau, parked the car on the south end of Borden Lake, and started paddling northward. Our goal was Lake Nemegosenda.

We made camp at the north end of Borden. It was swampy and full of giant mosquitoes. We had to go up a hillside, where it was windy, but barren of saplings that could be used for tent poles and stakes, so we hung the tent over a rope between two trees on about a ten-degree slope. It was sure a sorry camp.

The next day we portaged to a small lake and then to a larger lake. There we met Mickey, a Canadian forest ranger, and his two Indian boy helpers. Harold's fifth of 7 Crown gave us an immediate friend in Mickey. Mickey told the boys to pitch our tent for us, took one look at it and said, "Take it down and put my tent up for them."

After two days, Mickey and the boys left and he let us use his cabin. The first night was quite interesting. We heard what sounded like sawing logs all night. In the morning we found little piles of sawdust from holes in the logs that supported our beds – pine beetles! We walked the portage to Nemegosenda and decided that it was too swampy for us to negotiate carrying a canoe and our gear. The fishing was great where we were, so we decided to stay. We fished for great northern pike. The fish would strike a lure right after it hit the water, go deep, and wrap around a log on the bottom; it was either be quick or lose bait. We tried trolling for lake trout, but could not paddle the canoe fast enough to get results.

After a week we headed home. A lot of my mental cobwebs were swept away. I knew what I had to do. We had car trouble on the way home and could barely keep the car running; the distributor had slipped. When we got to Harold's house it was quite late, but I borrowed his 1951 Chrysler and drove out to see Jo.

I got my car fixed the next day and went "home." I told Mona about Jo, and told her that I wanted to leave. It was a painful, sobering time, and circumstances were such that I could not make an immediate break, so we were forced to go on living in the same house, but separately. One of the many problems we had was lack of money; and I was very hesitant about making a rash move.

At the same time, the thought of spiritual need was still fresh. I wanted a church home, but still had not found one. Jo was most helpful during my quest. She encouraged me, went to churches with me, but did not try to push me in any one direction.

3 – A Spiritual Find

North of Detroit is the city of Bloomfield Hills, a very wealthy community that has an England-oriented center, Cranbrook. Christ Church Cranbrook (Episcopal) was reputed to be a replica of an English cathedral. I went there one Sunday, mainly to see the architecture and artwork, though I still had an aversion to the Episcopal Church. The church was beautiful, and the music and choir were most inspiring. They were having Holy Communion that Sunday, and I joined in the worship.

At the beginning of Holy Communion, the Celebrant said, "Ye who do truly and earnestly repent you of your sins, and are in love and charity with your neighbors, and intend to lead a new life, following the commandments of God, and walking from henceforth in his holy ways; Draw near with faith, and take this holy Sacrament to your comfort; and make your confession to Almighty God, devoutly kneeling." *(Book of Common Prayer, page 75)* This was what I wanted: "to lead a new life, following the commandments of God, and walking in his holy ways."

I met Our Lord Jesus in that pew. I sensed His presence behind me at my right shoulder. I was filled with awe, yet felt quite calm, not frightened, except I was really afraid to turn around and look. I had found my Lord. I had found my church. What irony, that I had been so disdainful of the Episcopal Church before. I started going to Christ Church regularly, and really liked the prescribed order of worship and having the Scriptures read regularly on a schedule that covered the whole Bible.

Before long I encountered the other side of repentance. I would go to church and hear this voice in my mind: "It is blasphemy for you to be here with all these good people. Leave! You don't belong here."

I thought, "This can only be from Satan, trying to steal my salvation," and I resisted the voice. This happened Sunday after Sunday several times, and then ceased. ("Resist the devil and he will flee from you." *James 4:7, KJV)*

4 – Rebuilding Life

I enrolled for a reduced school schedule in the fall of '54 and was able to handle two classes and make up an incomplete in a third class. In October, Long Manufacturing decided to convert their stock accounting procedures to IBM computers. Jo was offered, but did not want, a typing job in the front office, and took lay-off instead. She quickly found a new job as a clerk/typist with Detroit Ball Bearing Company. I was given the choice of learning to program the computers or working as a technician testing clutches in the Engineering Lab. I took the technician job. It was a way to get into engineering and start using some of my education. After a few weeks I was asked to go on the drawing board designing clutches. This suited me much more than the laboratory work. I liked drafting, and soon discovered that I was a pretty good designer.

There is not much else to recount from the fall of 1954. Jo and I saw each other regularly, coped with new jobs, and agonized over how to handle our situation. Money was short, and that hampered us from making any abrupt moves.

Christmas Eve of 1954 was really neat. I took Jo to Christ Church for the midnight mass. I was sure that with her Pentecostal and Baptist background she would be repelled by a service so obviously Catholic. Surprise, surprise! She liked the service and the church. I told her that I had thought she would surely object. She said it was nothing new to her, that she had spent lots of time in Catholic churches with her neighbors. This was great! My newfound religion was not going to be an obstacle for us.

Early 1955 was difficult. My recovery was not going well. I was having trouble regulating medications. Thyroxin often made me hyper and I would have to take a suppressant to calm down. I asked Dr. Geitz, "How long will I have to take thyroxin?"

He replied, "For the rest of your life."

I did not like the sound of that.

My relationship with Jo also caused a lot of stress. I was still under the same roof with Mona, and my family disapproved of the situation. My father, Richard William Marshall, and fourteen-year-old sister, Sharon, were very critical of my plans for divorce. Mother was unhappy about the situation, but she understood the causes and was supportive. The strain was such that I was not able to keep up with work and school, and finally dropped all my classes except accounting.

I filed for divorce and moved out in June of 1955. Uncle Harold and Aunt Babs were very sympathetic with my situation; they had lived with us for six weeks and knew what my home conditions were like. They let me move in with them. Mona started a counter suit, and it looked like things were going to be bitter and drawn out. Through all of this I tried to keep on in school, but again wound up dropping more classes than I completed. And I quarreled with Dr. Geitz. "Why am I not getting any better?"

His reply was, "How long did it take you to get this way?"

"Three years."

"Alright, you give me three years to undo all the damage that you've done."

"Okay, fair enough."

Jo had problems with her job, but we were able to get her a new job in the Water Department of the City of Oak Park, the city where my father was mayor.

During this time I felt guilty about going all the way to Cranbrook for church when I was passing smaller churches that could probably have better used my support, so I started going to St. Margaret's in Hazel Park. The rector, Fr. Stanley Smith, was young, single, and a ham radio operator. We spent a lot of time together talking electronics, and in the process I told him my story. At that time the Episcopal Church opposed the remarriage of divorced persons. Stanley was very traditional and said he wanted to investigate the possibility of reconciliation. He met and talked with Mona, and became convinced that there was little or no hope of reconciliation. This allowed Stanley to accept my "seeing" Jo more readily.

On December 27th I was granted a divorce. After several sincere discussions, Mona dropped her counter suit and agreed to a settlement that gave her the house, custody of young Richard, and child support. I was given unlimited visiting rights with Richard, both at his home and away from it. We parted amicably. There would be a six-month wait before the divorce became final, but at last a major obstacle was overcome. My parents accepted the situation and there was harmony in the family again. Now Jo and I were faced with the real possibility of becoming married, and that added a rather serious dimension to our courtship.

There was a "looking to the future," however. I made a trip to my mother's hometown, Wiarton, Ontario, with Mother, Harold and Babs. There we came across a man staking out property on Lake Huron. I talked to him about the property and bought 100 feet of lake frontage for the sum of $300. This would be the start of several real estate ventures.

In January of 1956 I started a new job designing power steering gears. It was interesting work and involved new friends.

On March 25th, Palm Sunday, I was confirmed at St. Margaret's. Jo and I talked about her becoming confirmed. She said she would if and when we were married, but she said it would hurt too much if she went through the confirmation process and the marriage did not take place.

In August of 1956 I took a vacation trip to Toronto and stayed with a fraternity brother. This time away from Jo made me realize how much I wanted to marry her.

Stiff competition in the steering gear business brought about a layoff at the end of the year. Bob, our manager, took it upon himself to get jobs for those of us who were being laid off. He arranged an interview for me with Chrysler as a designer/draftsman. It sounded good – a top-notch company and more money. At the interview, to my surprise, I found they were more interested in me as an engineer than a designer/draftsman. I felt wonderfully blessed. It was a lot more money than I had ever made and I would be getting into electrical engineering.

5 – The Path Gets Rough

The stress of the divorce and our prolonged courtship began taking their toll. Jo and I had several disputes over some of my stated social and lifestyle expectations of a wife. I told her I aspired to go into politics and become socially prominent, and how desirable it was for me to have a complementary mate. That was not the lifestyle that Jo envisioned, and she forthrightly stated her doubts of being able to meet my expectations, which were really quite ridiculous. She didn't think she could, or wanted to, measure up. She wanted a quiet life, preferably in a little white cottage.

We came very close to breaking up permanently over another absolutely ridiculous thing. I wanted to join a flying club that was forming at school. I was sure Jo would not approve. To avoid a quarrel, I quit calling her for a couple of weeks. The flying club fell through. I was miserable with the separation and attempted to patch things up with Jo.

During the hiatus, Jo traded her pale green '53 Ford for a neat red '55 Thunderbird convertible and was starting to feel a new sense of independence. Her attitude toward me was like "Go to Jail, Do Not Pass Go, Do Not Collect $200," but at least she did let me start seeing her again. To one-up her red Thunderbird, I bought a new pink and white '57 one.

In May of 1957 we went to my fraternity's dinner dance at the Falcon Lounge in Northeast Detroit. While we were sitting at the bar after dinner, I asked Jo to marry me, and pressured her for a positive answer. She didn't say no, but she evaded giving me a definite answer. On my knees, I asked her again, and she finally said, "Oh, I suppose so."

I stood up and told the gathering that I had an announcement to make. "Jo and I are going to be married." There was much applause and many congratulations. Jo looked a little nonplussed and said that she really hadn't had enough time to get used to the idea.

At that same time I was doubly blessed in a rather unexpected way. I had prayed continuously to be able to stop taking thyroxin. Much to my and Dr. Geitz' surprise, my blood pressure started going up and *I was able to quit all medications*.

6 – Our Union

Jo felt very strongly that our marriage should have a firm foundation. We believed that we should go to the same church, and she wanted us to be married in that church. The Episcopal Church had just changed the canons to allow remarriage with a Bishop's consent. We talked with Stanley about our desire to be married in the Church, and he arranged for us to meet with the bishop's advisory committee. We resolved that if we were denied permission we would look at our whole situation in terms of God's will for us.

We went to St. Paul's Cathedral in Detroit, and there we met with three very stern-looking dowagers. They questioned us thoroughly about our past, our intentions, and our assurance that our marriage would not lead to another divorce.

Within two weeks we heard from Stanley that the bishop had given us his consent. As far as I know, we were the first couple to receive such consent in the Diocese of Michigan. We immediately started to plan for our marriage. Part of the marriage process was meeting with Fr. Stanley for pre-marital counseling. Stanley strongly emphasized the need for a couple to say their prayers together every day, and reminded us of St. Paul's admonition, "Do not let the sun go down on your anger." (*Ephesians 4:26, RSV*) We agreed to abide by these teachings.

The next important step was to find a place to live. There was a housing shortage in the Detroit area, but we did find a nice, furnished, basement apartment in a three-family house in Ferndale. The apartment was nicely finished, comfortable, and even had a fireplace. There was a bonus feature for Jo, also. The son of the couple that lived in the upstairs unit was Harold Boatright, a performer and composer of classical music who was associated with the Curtis Institute of Music in Philadelphia. We got together with them whenever he visited his parents, and had lively conversations about music.

On July 20th we were joined in Holy Matrimony at St. Margaret's Church, Hazel Park, Michigan. We scheduled the wedding early in the morning, because the church did not have air conditioning. It was ninety degrees that morning. It was near nine o'clock and my best man, Harold Haupt, had not shown up. We called his house and his mother said that he had already left. At nine o'clock Stanley came into the vesting room and said, "We can't wait any longer. We'll just have to go ahead without Harold." Just then, Harold pulled into the parking lot. He had been sick at his stomach and had to stop on the way to church. We started late, but we did get started. Stanley, Harold, and I went into the church, and the organist started the processional. Mother and Dad were there, but Sharon was away for the summer and missed the event.

Jo started down the aisle on her father's arm. She was a thing of beauty, looking like a fine china doll, radiant in her waltz length white dress. I wondered, "Is this real? What have I done to deserve her? Is something going to happen to stop it?"

During the procession a nasty mosquito landed in the middle of Jo's back. Many from the congregation said they were tempted to get up and smack it. During the Communion, Jo and I were kneeling at the altar rail and it was so hot that the perspiration ran from my forehead, fell on her dress, and left a large wet spot. Despite the minor irritations, we were officially joined "as one" and we went into the parish hall for the breakfast reception as man and wife.

Jo was not able to get time off work, so we had to settle for a two-day honeymoon in middle Michigan. We followed the Lake Huron coast around the thumb. We stopped in Grindstone City and saw the massive millstones covering the beach, leftover from the era when Grindstone City supplied stone wheels for gristmills all over the country. From there we went around Saginaw Bay and checked into a motel in East Tawas. It was getting late in the evening and we had not had dinner. We started looking for a restaurant and spotted a police car parked alongside the road. We pulled up and asked the officer, "Where can we find a good restaurant?"

"Do you like barbecue?"

"Yes."

"Follow me."

Off we went down the highway. Pretty soon we were going 75 miles an hour on the 55 mph highway, and I started to wonder. Was he suckering me in for a speeding ticket? I had past experience with the prejudice city police had against sports cars and their drivers. But he was just getting us there quickly, and it turned out to be a good restaurant.

I'm not sure what the problem was – timidity, tiredness, too much barbecue, or just plain being afraid – but things were rather clumsy on our wedding night. Many times afterward we thought we probably would not have married if we had not waited before having intercourse. Many, many times we thanked God that we did wait.

The next day we followed the coastline to Rogers City, then turned inland and headed for home.

We settled into our new life and new home on July 22nd. I now affectionately knew Bernice and Neil Golden as "Ma" and "Pa."

I was on probation from school because I had dropped some classes after midterm and had to take failing grades, so I decided it might be a good idea to take off from school for the first year of our marriage.

We spent the rest of the summer pursuing the outdoors activities we liked to do together. We picnicked and swam at several state parks, went to the cider mills in the fall, and ice-skated in the winter. It was great.

Things got rather nasty during the fall of 1957. Jo came down with Asiatic flu and was extremely sick. She had severe headaches, and I used to sit and hold her head in my lap, trying to give her some form of comfort. We got through the fall and celebrated our first Christmas together in our own home, and awaited a New Year – 1958.

Jo and I both had vacation time coming, so we packed up my T-bird and set off for a belated honeymoon in February. We had planned to go down the west coast of Florida, visit my Aunt Gertrude in Dade City, visit former Oak Park neighbors on Sanibel Island, then go to Miami and take a ship to Cuba.

On the way down we visited Mammoth Cave in Kentucky. We took the long tour and had lunch in the cave's big underground dining hall, called the Snowball Room because of snowball-like formations on the ceiling. The constant 54-degree temperature was monotonous and left me feeling chilled. I was glad when we got back outside, and felt that it would be a long time before I ever went into a cave for that long again.

We had a good visit with Aunt Gertrude and my fifteen-year-old cousin, Glen. We all went to the Greek community at Tarpon Springs and feasted on their lamb dishes, Greek salad, and baklava. Jo was thoroughly captivated by the pottery they had for sale and we bought what we could afford, a large glazed vase embellished with mythological figures.

Florida was experiencing a horrid freeze. Fruit trees were bare and the ground was carpeted orange and yellow with fallen fruit. We went on to Sanibel Island, a place renowned for shell collecting, but we couldn't find a motel with heat. Most of the places depended on portable electric heaters, and they were all being used, so we left the island on the last ferry. We spent the night in Clewiston, on the south shore of Lake Okeechobee, watched the weather reports on TV, and saw oil fires in irrigation trenches that had been set by farmers trying to save their vegetable plants. Miami had been stripped of blankets and heaters to relieve the people suffering from the cold in Cuba, and many places were without heat of any kind. We abandoned our plans to travel further south, and instead set off for the east coast of Florida.

We followed A1A up the coast toward Cape Canaveral. A rocket launch was scheduled that day and we thought we would try to see it. The traffic was so heavy in Melbourne we missed the launch, so we headed for Daytona Beach. It was windy, cloudy, and fifty degrees, and Jo just loved it. She walked the beach with the wind blowing in her face. Then we spent some time driving the T-bird on the hard packed sand. From Daytona we went to Ormond by the Sea, another beach that Jo really loved. Again, no heated accommodations anywhere, so we continued north toward Jacksonville.

Jo really loved the shore wilderness at St. Augustine; it resonated with her love of the outdoors and the wild. There was very little development at that time, and much of the shoreline was covered with saw grass, sea oats, and scrubby trees. The area was basically a summer haven, and everything was closed for the winter. Night was coming fast, so we pushed on to Jacksonville. We found a motel, but they were out of propane gas, so, no heat, but they did say they had a load of gas coming in later and if we wanted to go eat, they would call us at the restaurant. They recommended The Lobster House, a lovely place on the St. John's River between the two southern bridges. We dined on lobster and sipped whiskey sours until the motel called us around midnight.

The next day we went to Waycross, Georgia and spent a good part of the day in the Okeefenokee Swamp. From there we went to Alexander City, Alabama and spent the night. Alabama and the whole Midwest were covered with snow, so I decided the next day to drive as long as I could. By midnight we were near Fort Wayne, Indiana, and I was getting pretty tired. We found a McDonald's that was open and I bought five cups of coffee to go. I lined up the coffee on top of the dashboard and drank a cup about every forty miles.

It took us twenty-three hours to cover the 930 miles home, but we made it. We pulled into Jo's parents' place, woke them up, went inside and told Ma, "The car is full of fruit. Take it out so it won't freeze. We're going to bed, we'll see you later." Then we went into Jo's old room and crashed.

Although our trip had not been anything like what we had planned, it was wonderful. It was the honeymoon that we did not have.

After we returned from Florida, Jo and her mother both started confirmation classes at St. Margaret's. Jo and Ma were confirmed on April 13, 1958, First Sunday After Easter.

In June of '58 we bought our first piece of furniture – a new Baldwin console piano. Jo had continued her piano studies at Detroit Conservatory of Music up till the time we were married. She was an excellent pianist. I loved to hear her play, and wanted her to be able to carry on with her music. We went to Smiley Brothers to look at some used pianos. For some reason, I didn't like any of them. But we both liked the new Baldwin, so I said, "We'll take it." Jo was thrilled. We told the salesman about the narrow stairway leading to our apartment. He said, "Our people can handle that alright." And they did.

Later we decided that we could afford for Jo to quit work to study humanities at Wayne State University. She started in the fall and did very well in her classes.

We had all talked about the flying club fiasco, and it turned out that Jo was not opposed to my learning to fly. Pa put me in touch with an instructor through a man he worked with, and I started taking flying lessons. In December I joined Eximious Flying Club with my boss Joe Littmann, and got my pilot's license a year later. How foolish I had been not to trust Jo enough to tell her what I wanted to do a year earlier!

7 – We Begin a Family

Jo became pregnant with our first child in the fall of '58. Life started to move faster for us now. It was imperative that we have better housing than the basement apartment. At that time my dad became City Manager in Madison Heights, and my parents moved into a newly developed neighborhood there. We found a nice, new, three-bedroom brick home in the same area. Dad lent us some money and we made the down payment. In April of 1959 we moved into our own new home on Jerry Avenue. We bought kitchen and bedroom furniture, and for the living room we borrowed furniture that my parents had bought for their recreation room.

One of Jo's coworkers gave us an orange tabby male kitten that we named Tobie. He was the first of many cats. Tobie left one night and did not come back. We think he was stolen. Shortly after, Jo and I walked past a pet store and a little brown tabby kitten tried to squeeze out of the cage to get to us. We bought her and named her Puff. We never again went for a long period of time without a cat.

I was back in school, carrying nine hours of classes and getting good grades.

Jo had a problem during her pregnancy. She developed phlebitis in one leg and had to be hospitalized for a week until the clot dissolved and a proper dosage of blood thinners could be determined.

Gerald Keith was born to us on June 30th. There were problems, however. He had a cleft lip and palate and would need surgery. This was more than I thought I could handle. However, my boss, Joe, had a girl born with a cleft lip, and at the age of six she showed hardly any trace of the deformity. Joe was able to give me the hope and courage I needed to go on.

The next day I was passing out cigars and candy when Joe came to me and said, "I need to talk to you in private." Gerald had suffered a cranial hemorrhage and died. He was spared the pain of surgeries and recoveries. The technician working for me had lost two children, and I often thought I could not handle such a loss. Now I was faced with it without any warning.

We got through the burial arrangements with the help of Fr. Smith and a very compassionate funeral director. One thing I felt bad about was the fact that we had not had Gerald baptized, especially when we knew he had problems. To compensate, I went to the cathedral and bought a silver cross to place in his hands. I came out of the cathedral and found a $15 parking ticket on my car. I felt just a little snake bit but I accepted that as a part of life also. During his very brief life Gerald taught us that we were capable of handling, with God's help, more than we thought we could.

The doctors all said that we should be able to have more children, so we began looking ahead. We left Gerald's room as we had prepared it. It was a soft yellow, very bright and warm. It was a place that felt good. Puff, spent a lot of time in that room.

All along this way, my spirituality was growing, and Stanley suggested that I consider going to the Bishop's School to prepare for ordination as an unpaid worker-priest. The thought appealed to me. I recalled a time in my childhood when I thought I wanted to become a minister, but thought I would never be able to prepare and preach sermons.

The fall of 1959 found me back in school, and Jo and I were busy making our house a home. We added a stereo, which gave us the music that was so important to us, and other pieces of furniture. And then we got hit with the flu again. It hit me particularly hard, settling in my chest and causing a severe case of bronchitis. The wracking cough was endless and painful. I took the maximum amount of codeine allowed by law, and was sipping whiskey and chewing raw onions to try to numb my throat. I asked Dr. Geitz to put me in the hospital, but he said, "The hospitals are so full they are for the dying only, and you have not reached that stage yet." It took six weeks to get over the coughing and I lost the whole semester of school.

Things were looking up for us in 1960. I was back in school. Jo was selling Avon and giving piano lessons. She really enjoyed being able to teach and have her own business. I redeemed the sin of buying a Thunderbird while working for Chrysler by getting a new metallic dark green Valiant. It had a totally new body that was rust proof, with Italian-inspired style. It was a really neat little car. My Thunderbird needed rusted rocker panels replaced, but I was able to sell it "as is" through a want ad. Jo's Thunderbird developed engine problems and was also rusting. We sold it to an electrician I knew and took a 1954 Ford two door hardtop as partial payment.

I finished all of my classes and we spent the summer with family and friends, going swimming, and taking long drives in the country. We became involved in politics, despite Jo's previously stated aversion to such a life. I was elected Precinct Delegate, became Party Chairman for Madison Heights, and we both plunged wholehearted into the 1960 presidential campaign. At the end of the process I decided that, unlike my father, I was not really suited for the political life, but I was totally pleased with Jo's enthusiastic support and involvement.

In September, Jo was pregnant again. We did a lot of praying for that baby. The pregnancy was not easy because of fluid retention, but Jo got through it, and I got through all of my classes in school. Graduation was on June 4th of 1961 in Cobo Hall, part of Detroit's downtown civic center. Jo was one very pregnant lady, watching as I walked up to get my Bachelor of Science degree in Electrical Engineering. President Lawrence said quite softly, "Well, Dick, we wondered if you would ever make it," as he handed me the degree certificate. It took eleven years to get that degree but I made it with a lot of help and encouragement from Jo.

June 20, 1961 was a day to remember. Stella Delaney, Jo's doctor, was scheduled for a trip to Europe and Jo was not coming along very fast. Stella had me take Jo to Grace Hospital so they could induce labor. On the way home I stopped at Dad's office to tell him the news. He was on his way out when I arrived, and he was flushed and very short of breath. He said he was having trouble breathing and was on his way to the doctor. I said, "You better let me take you there." On the way out of the parking lot his brakes failed momentarily and we almost wound up in heavy traffic; I was glad that it happened to me and not to him. I got Dad to Dr. Bronson's office and found out he was having a major coronary attack. Dad was taken by ambulance to Henry Ford Hospital in Dearborn, Michigan, and I went to their house to get Mother.

After I got my folks settled in at Ford Hospital, I called Grace Hospital. Dr. Delaney got on the phone and said, "Where in the hell have you been? We've been looking all over hell's half acre for you. You have a baby girl, and everything is fine."

A young lady had entered our world. I got to Grace Hospital and almost right away a nurse asked, "Can you give us the baby's name?"

Jo and I had not yet settled on a name, so we started saying names aloud, to try them out. One street over from Jerry was Jenifer Avenue. I saw that with my mind's eye, and said, "Jenifer."

Jo said, "With one 'n' or two?"

I said, "One 'n'." Jennifer was in pretty common use because of the movie star Jennifer Jones, but we wanted something different. Elaine had already been considered, but it didn't seem right as a first name. There we had it: Jenifer Elaine Marshall. Bright red, with a pointy-head, which the nurses all said would go away and become normal.

    After a week, we brought Jenifer home and put her in the room we had prepared for Gerald. Puff immediately adopted her. It seemed like she had been waiting for two years for someone to fill that room and her life. Ma and Pa now became Granny and Gramper. "Granny" later was shortened to "Gran."

8 – The Horizon Broadens

Poor car sales in 1961 were causing problems at Chrysler. There was a change in our management and I lost out on a promotion that I felt I had earned, and badly wanted. I left Chrysler in August to organize and head a product engineering group at Howell Industries, one of the suppliers I worked with at Chrysler. As Chief Engineer in a small company I had a good salary, but became restless. I felt that all I could do at Howell was make money, and I wanted more challenge from my work than that. I had a fresh engineering degree in my pocket, the desire to go to graduate school, and the desire to enter the electronics field. I prayed about the situation, then talked to people in the alumni office at Lawrence Tech. They gave me a publication that listed educational and job opportunities for graduates. I picked the company I was most interested in, Battelle Memorial Institute in Columbus, Ohio, and sent them a resume.

In March of 1962 I received an offer from Battelle and was accepted into graduate school at Ohio State University. I would be working on the control systems for a massive radio telescope to be built for the U.S. Navy in Virginia. It sounded like a great opportunity, so we put our house up for sale and moved into an apartment in Columbus. For recreation we bought a small boat with a 5 horsepower motor, which we used for a while there, then took up to my parents' cottage in Canada.

The promise of a desirable career would not last. The Navy telescope project was canceled, and our department had to rely on minor study contracts to maintain employment. I gave up graduate school to spend time looking for another job.

That winter we almost lost Jo. She appeared to be having an early-pregnancy miscarriage and started hemorrhaging. We had a severe ice storm and the roads were so bad we could not get an ambulance. I took Jenifer to the lady next door, and drove Jo to the hospital. The roads were covered with a glaze of ice. It was a blessing there was no other traffic. I prayed all the way that we would get there in time, not have an accident, and that Jo would be alright.

When we arrived, there was nobody at the emergency entrance, and I had to go in to get someone to take Jo inside. She was taken to surgery and started going under. They tried to give her blood, but the unit was faulty and they had to get more. Valuable time was being lost.

She heard them say, "We've lost her," and later recounted that she was out of her body, floating above the table, looking down, and able to see everything going on. She said it was bright and warm where she was, and felt really good, but she felt she needed to get back to take care of Jenifer and me. And then, she returned to her body, which she said was both difficult and painful. It took several weeks, but Jo did recover fully.

My search for a new job finally bore fruit. In January of '63 I was hired as a flight test instrumentation engineer at North American Aviation. It was wonderful. I was working with high performance aircraft, gaining electronics experience, and taking advantage of an excellent company school. Our work was primarily on the RA5C Vigilante, a twin-engine supersonic reconnaissance plane that had been a bomber. I would get off work at three o'clock, get Jo and Jenifer, and we would spend our afternoons watching the Vigilantes take off and land at Port Columbus. They were sleek, fast, and loud. It was like having a picnic and air show every day.

But again I was caught by contract cancellations. The Navy decided to terminate the Vigilante program in November. I was offered a transfer to California to work on the Apollo spacecraft, but we decided that was too far to move.

There was also sadness. Puff got out of the apartment one day and ran away. We found her body days later alongside the nearby freeway.

At this same time, a manager that I knew at Ford Motor Company in Dearborn called me and asked me to work for him in the Advanced Features Section, inventing and designing new control features for cars of the future. They offered a good salary increase, and we still had the house in Madison Heights, so we decided to go back to Detroit in December. Then we got a call from the real estate agent. Our house had been sold. We did not try to block the sale, because the house was a long way from Dearborn, and we felt we should buy another house closer to work. However, there was a building strike in Detroit at the time and housing was impossible to find, especially so close to Christmas. So, I commuted from Columbus to Dearborn on weekends and stayed with my parents through the week.

Misfortune struck again in March. Someone set fire to the downstairs area of our apartment unit one night while I was in Michigan. Jo and Jen barely got out in time. Jo picked Jenifer up, put a blanket over her head, and carried her next door. Neighbors took them in and called the fire department. We don't know if the fire was the result of a botched burglary attempt or racially motivated terrorism. There was a lot of racial unrest in Columbus at that time. The perpetrator was never caught. It was obvious we could not stay in Columbus any longer. We lost our living room furniture, except the stereo and the piano, which only suffered smoke damage. We put the furniture that was saved in storage and moved in with Jo's parents in Warren.

Earlier in the year it had become apparent that Jo's teeth were going bad, and it looked like she would need full dentures. An oral surgeon in Columbus did a very poor job on her, taking too much tissue from the jaw, and sedating her so heavily that she wound up in the hospital. Fortunately, by being in Warren we were now able to get her work completed by her previous dentist.

We finally got a good apartment in Royal Oak and moved there in June. Work went well. Ford management was impressed with what could be done with electronics. One of the things I designed was the circuitry and hardware that made it possible to operate a speed control from buttons on the steering wheel. I put the first one on a 1964 Thunderbird, and was most gratified years later to see the concept appear on all cars. Despite the fact that I was well paid and well liked, I did not get much satisfaction from my work. I missed the emphasis on quality and being on the cutting edge of technology. In short, I missed the aerospace industry.

In July of '64 a team of recruiters from The Boeing Company came to Detroit seeking engineers to staff the Saturn space program. I went for an interview. When I got back home, Jo said, "Well?"

"I think I've got a job."
"Where? New Orleans?"
"No, Huntsville, Alabama."
"Huntsville, Alabama???"
"Yes."

1964 was another year of racial unrest, especially in Alabama, and Jo couldn't understand why I wanted to go there. However, ten years earlier, when I went to Florida with my mother and young Richard, I stopped to see Guntersville Dam, 25 miles east of Huntsville. I was so impressed with the beauty of the Tennessee River Valley that I told Mother I thought it would be a wonderful place to live if there was ever a way to make a living. An offer came through from Boeing and now there was a way. I told Jo, "Let me take you there, show you the place, and then we'll decide." We left Jenifer with Gran and Gramper in early August and went there.

Jo fell in love with Huntsville and suggested that I leave her there to find a place to live while I went back to Royal Oak and made moving arrangements. I told her, "That car is not going to head north unless you are sitting next to me."

Between the time of my interview with Boeing and their offer, Ford had given me a promotion and a very substantial raise. Jo confessed later that she wanted to stay in Huntsville because she was afraid I would turn the Boeing offer down, because of the smaller salary. I didn't turn the offer down, and we got ready to move. I recalled my "Buck Rogers" days in childhood and all the time I spent drawing rocket ships and playing rocket ship, and wondered if maybe that had been a peek into the future.

9 – We Become Southerners

We arrived in Huntsville on October 4th, 1964. It was cold and rainy, not the sunny warmth we expected. The motel room was cold. They hadn't turned the heat on. We did not have a place to live, and a van full of our belongings would arrive in a week.

I started work on Tuesday, the 6th. Huntsville was growing rapidly, because of the buildup for the Saturn space program, and it was difficult to get housing. Jo would go to the newspaper office in the morning and get the paper right after it came out. We would then have time to see two, maybe three houses that morning and the rest would already be rented. Those we were able to see were pretty sorry and we just didn't feel like settling for the first thing available.

A loving God was taking care of us, though. We called a real estate office a few days later about a house, and were told that the agent was not available. We left a phone number and asked to be called when he became available, which no one else had thought to do. The agent called us late that afternoon. We found out later that he had been watching the World Series and did not want to be disturbed. He took us to see a new brick house that had not been lived in. The house had been sold under a VA contract, the deal fell through, and government rules prevented its resale for a year, so we were able to get a new house, a nice house, beside a mountain in northwest Huntsville. By the time the moving van got to town, we were ready to move in. People we were acquainted with in Huntsville could not believe how fortunate we were.

After we had settled in we found out that Huntsville usually welcomed autumn with two weeks of cold, nasty, wet weather. Then it turned into a beautiful Indian summer. It was warm and sunny right up until Christmas. On Christmas Eve I was in shirtsleeves, swinging Jenifer on her new swing set. After Christmas, winter hit with cold winds and light snow.

Right behind our house was a large ranch house with separate guest cottages. The house was being used as St. Christopher's Episcopal Church. The guest cottages were used for Sunday School. It was nice to be able to walk across our backyard to go to church. The rector, Fr. Charles McKimmon, was a young single priest. It reminded me of St. Margaret's and Fr. Stanley Smith. Most of the members were Boeing and IBM employees and we fit in right away.

Once again we were moving ahead at a good pace. I put air conditioning in our new '64 Dodge Dart, and made a sand box in the backyard for Jenifer. The sandbox quickly became a nesting place for black widow spiders and a litter box for neighborhood cats, so it did not last very long.

We had long talked about getting a dog, and decided we'd like to have a collie. Through want ads we found the Hamilton's – Bill, Betty, and their two boys, Jimmy and David. Betty raised and showed collies, and had a beautiful tricolor female puppy for sale. We couldn't resist, so Peigi joined the family, and we became very good friends with the Hamilton's. Jo spent a lot of time with Betty, learning about breeding and showing collies. A friend of the Hamilton's then gave us a lovely brown tabby kitten we named Kitty. Our family was now complete. Jo chose Elsinore as her kennel name, and Jen and I helped her design a logo with a collie head superimposed on a castle tower.

Richard gave us a surprise at the beginning of the New Year. He had turned eighteen and graduated high school. Jo and I talked about putting him through college at University of Alabama in Huntsville, if he wanted to come to Huntsville, but before I could call him, he called to tell us that he had enlisted in U. S. Army Intelligence. He went to language school in Monterey, California and was posted to Chitose, Hokkaido, Japan as an interpreter, monitoring radio transmissions from communist countries.

I enrolled in graduate school at UAH in the spring, and started taking the mathematics classes I needed to enter their master's program. Then we bought a new 15-foot fiberglass boat with a folding top, and became Tennessee River rats. We trailered the boat to different places on the Tennessee and Elk Rivers during 1965 and thoroughly explored the area by water.

Meanwhile, St. Christopher's moved to a new building on Pulaski Pike, about a half mile from us, and established a kindergarten. Huntsville public schools did not have kindergartens, so many of the churches opened their own. We enrolled Jenifer in September, and bought a lovely new maroon Dodge Polara station wagon for Jo, so she could chauffeur kids and dogs.

One warm, sunny weekend afternoon I was studying for fall term finals when Jen came into the den. "Daddy, please come and play with me."

"I can't, honey. I've got homework to do."

Mournfully, she said, "You've always got homework to do. You never have any time to play with me."

I gulped. Later I went into the bathroom, looked into the mirror and asked myself, "What are you doing to your family and yourself?" I wasn't really interested in the studies, and the prospect of earning more money was not sufficient motivation. I finished the term, but did not enroll for the winter term.

Jo used to walk Peigi in the open fields north of our neighborhood. On one of her walks she came across Cedar Point, a new subdivision, and saw a sprawling ranch house on the eastern edge. She took Jen and me to see it. We all loved the place. It was beautiful. The exterior was reclaimed brick from a hundred- year-old hotel in Montgomery. The house had three bedrooms, two baths, formal living and dining rooms, a laundry cove, a separate dinette, a dream kitchen, a large family room with walnut finished tongue and groove walls and one whole wall of brick with a fireplace, a walled carport with a utility room, and a patio with a brick barbecue pit. This was no ordinary house. It surpassed everything in the subdivision and anything that we thought we could afford. Jo asked me, "How much do you think it is?"

"I don't know, probably twenty-seven, five." Beyond our reach. We only had fifteen hundred in the bank. The house was not quite finished and it wasn't being worked on.

I came home from work one day and Jo said, "You know the house in Cedar Point?"

"Yes."

"We can have it for twenty five thousand, seven fifty, and they'll take fifteen hundred down."

I couldn't believe what I was hearing. Something like that in booming Huntsville seemed impossible.

Jo went on. "I walked over to the house with Peigi. The real estate agent was there, and he asked me, 'Are you interested in this house?' I said, 'Yes, but I don't think we can afford it.' He said, 'Let's see if we can work something out.'" He gave Jo the price and told her that fifteen hundred dollars would handle it. The developer had been building the house for himself, but merged with a larger company and moved to Birmingham. The house had not been built with VA-FHA progress inspections and could only be financed with a conventional mortgage. There would be a higher interest rate than FHA, but that was okay with us. We made the deal, and they finished the house. ***God had totally blessed and enabled our move to Huntsville.***

We closed on our house on the 25th of January, 1966. It had snowed eleven inches the night before, and only brave fools from the North would try to drive on Huntsville's snowy streets. When we got downtown we had to drive on sidewalks because of all the abandoned cars on the streets.

We moved in ten days later. What a mess. A hard freeze had frozen our pipes. Several workmen were trying to thaw the pipes and had tracked mud everywhere, inside and out. But we were there, it was ours, no more renting, and it was beautiful. Jo was doubly happy because we now we had our own place and she could adapt it for raising collies.

In April of '66 we decided to quit trailing the boat, and docked it at Snug Harbor on Guntersville Lake on the Tennessee River. The Hamilton's used the same marina, so we joined them nearly every weekend for fishing, picnicking, and water skiing. We felt *truly blessed.*

Late spring saw the promise of new life for us; Jo was pregnant. Things had gone so well with Jenifer that we had little apprehension. Everything was going well at work, and we spent the rest of 1966 enjoying our home, our boat, our animals, our ongoing exploration of Alabama and Tennessee, and going to Redstone Arsenal to watch test firings of Saturn V rocket engines.

Gramper retired from Chrysler in the fall. Gran and Gramper sold their house in Warren and bought a forty-acre farm with a stone house near LaRussel, Missouri. Part of the farm was a forest of mature black oak trees, so they named the farm "Black Oaks." Gran was back in her home state and living near one of her sisters in Miller, Missouri.

It was quite exciting living in Cedar Point. At night we could hear wild cats howling on the mountain and would find large cat tracks in the mud by the pond in the meadow. The subdivisions in north Huntsville were relatively new and small, and were surrounded by active farms. Occasionally animals would wander into the neighborhood, and we wouldn't know where they came from. One day a small herd of pigs came down the hill at the entrance of the subdivision. Then there was a mule that would watch Jenifer eating breakfast, and two ponies that drank from our birdbath. Most exciting was the day we had eight cows in our yard. That just about drove Peigi crazy. I let her loose to see what she would do, and she immediately started to herd them. She moved them into an adjoining creek bed and drove them toward the farms. An hour or so later a very muddy dog came back acting very proud of herself. We were amazed at how strong her herding instinct was and how good she was at doing it.

10 – Tragedy Strikes Again

1967 was just nine days old when Kenneth Stuart was born. He was a lovely blond child, looked like an angel. We brought him home from the hospital after a week and he was doing just fine. However, the pediatrician had changed his formula when he left the hospital, and he quickly became severely constipated. His stomach became so badly distended that we rushed him to the hospital. Remembering our experience with Gerald, we called Fr. McKimmon and had him baptize Kenneth at the hospital. They started treating him and sent us home. We called later to see how things were and the doctor said, "You better get here as soon as possible." We got to the hospital and found that our angel had gone home to heaven after just nine days here. Subsequent examination showed that he had an intestinal problem, Hirschsprung's disease, and that he had died from peritonitis resulting from an intestinal perforation. The death was hard for us to take. When we tried, we could perhaps see a sense of mercy in Gerald's death, but we didn't feel any of that with Kenneth. Jenifer, just five and a half years old, was broken-hearted and bewildered by the loss of her brother. I never reached the point of accepting Kenneth's death.

Nine days into our grief, the nation and the world were shocked by the Apollo I tragedy. On January 27th the spacecraft caught fire and the three astronauts inside, Virgil "Gus" Grissom, Edward White, and Roger Chaffee, burned to death. On top of our personal loss, we now were suffering from the communal loss.

Shortly thereafter we suffered another loss. Jenifer came up behind Peigi one day and startled her. Peigi snarled and lunged at her. Fortunately, she recognized Jen at the last moment and did not attack, but Jenifer was terrified. We took Peigi to the vet and learned she was going blind. Rather than risk someone being seriously injured, we regretfully had Peigi put to sleep.

Looking back, I find it remarkable the way Jo handled adversity and grief. She would lick her wounds, heal, and then go ahead without looking back.

During World War II her father was drafted into the army. They received so little support from the government that Jo's mother had to work and leave Jo with relatives. Jo's diet was poor and she developed severe anemia that resulted in soft teeth. Then, early in high school she was afflicted with rheumatic fever, suffered the loss of her front teeth, and had a residual heart murmur. Despite these setbacks, Jo continued her studies of classical piano and voice, and played bass clarinet in the Warren High School band.

In April of 1967 we got Misty, a lovely blue merle collie puppy, and Jo planned to breed her.

11 – Picking up the Pieces

After the Apollo fire, the many detractors of the space program were calling for its cancellation. However, because of the commitment that President John F. Kennedy had made, "to put a man on the moon by 1970," people from all walks of life saw the program as a memorial to him that therefore could not very well be canceled, despite the calls from opposing groups to halt the risk and expense. To better ensure success of the Apollo/Saturn mission, NASA gave The Boeing Company a massive Systems Engineering and Integration contract to cover the whole spacecraft and launch vehicle system. Prior to that, Boeing was responsible for the S1C first stage booster only. This new contract assured that many of us would stay in Huntsville and not be transferred to Cape Kennedy to support S1C operations. I was transferred to Systems Engineering and gained broad experience on the electrical systems of the whole space vehicle. On November 9th NASA carried off the first unmanned Saturn V flight and Command Module reentry test. It was a success. The program was back on track.

In September of 1967 Jenifer started elementary school at Evangel School, a grades 1 through 12 Christian private school. The public schools were overcrowded and many children had not been to kindergarten. Kindergarten kids were academically far ahead of children the same age who had not been to kindergarten. We were pleased that Jenifer was going to receive a spiritual as well as an academic education in a school with a small student-to-teacher ratio.

During 1968 I had three different job assignments. The space program was progressing right on schedule and we had four successful Saturn/Apollo missions.

Jo was totally involved with the collies. She arranged breeding for Misty, but Misty would not cooperate. It turned out she had a uterine obstruction that made her unable to breed. We could have exchanged her for another bitch, but by now she had become a family pet, so we kept her. Not to be dismayed, Jo started looking for another bitch. Her quest took her to Florence Cummings, a well-known breeder in Oklahoma. Dottie Kennedy, a friend of Betty Hamilton, was going there to get a dog, and she invited Jo and Jen to go with her. Along the way they all stayed at Gran and Gramper's place. Jo brought home a lovely sable lady that we called Sheila. Sheila not only had looks, she had personality, was a very lively dog, and loved us thoroughly. I heard that Jen had a good time sleeping in the back of Dottie's station wagon with two collies.

12 – Changes

1969 was a big year, not only for NASA, but also for the Marshall's. Apollo 11 landed on the moon on our twelfth wedding anniversary, July 20. We had met John F. Kennedy's deadline with more than a year to spare. Boeing was awarded the contract to build the Manned Lunar Roving Vehicle (LRV) and I was assigned to that project with responsibility for instrumentation and power. There were only about two hundred people assigned to the Lunar Rover, so we all had major responsibilities.

In May of '68 Richard married a Japanese girl, Keiko, while stationed in Chitose. They came to visit us in March of '69, along with their infant son Richard Douglas (Dickie). We were now grandparents. Keiko was quiet and reserved, but we sensed she was also strong willed.

They visited again in July of 1970, while in the states for Richard to receive additional training. This would be the last time that we would see Dickie.

Richard was taken from his normal duties in intelligence and assigned to combat duty in Viet Nam. Because of his religious convictions, he applied for conscientious objector status. He was then assigned to civil affairs duty, but, as a condition, he would not be allowed to re-enlist at the end of his term. His army career would be ended. Pairs of soldiers were sent into Viet Nam villages, to teach and assist the villagers to become self-governing. It was dangerous duty. The villages were Viet Nam during the day, but Viet Cong at night. All of the soldiers Richard was paired with were killed, but not while serving with him. It was a ***miracle*** that he survived without even being wounded. He was awarded the Bronze Star for meritorious service for the work he accomplished in Viet Nam.

Richard's enlistment ended in 1971 and he was sent to Oakland, California for discharge processing. Keiko refused to go back to the States with him. Richard was quite sick from an amoebic infection and went home to Michigan for three months to recover, then returned to Japan in an unsuccessful attempt to salvage his marriage. Keiko stayed in Japan and subsequently divorced him. Richard was so traumatized by his experiences in Viet Nam and the loss of his marriage, that after two months he went to San Francisco and stayed there for a year and a half, until he regained some perspective. He then returned to Michigan to pursue a business interest.

Dad retired from his job as City Manager in Madison Heights. Harold and I helped Mother and Dad move to Dade City, Florida. They kept the cottage in Canada and became snowbirds. It was a good arrangement for us. They would spend a week with us during their spring and fall treks, and we had a place to stay near Tampa.

Jenifer was gaining so much Bible knowledge that St. Christopher's Sunday School just wasn't challenging enough for her, so we started going to Church of the Nativity, the big antebellum church downtown. It was a difficult decision. We felt like we were running out on the folks at St. Christopher's. What we couldn't foresee was the impact the move would have on our lives later.

Again we were expecting a baby. Ian Douglas was born on December 3rd, the same birthday as Richard Brian's. During the delivery Jo remembers hearing Dr. Lary say, "We're going to have to do a little midwiffery here. It looks like we have a water head baby." Ian was hydrocephalic and also had a heart problem. We talked with his doctors, a pediatrician and a neurosurgeon. The situation was not impossible, but would be difficult. We resolved to do whatever we could to nurture that little life. We had Fr. Emile Joffrion, the rector of Nativity, baptize and pray for Ian right away. Then we experienced *a miracle*; the size and pressure in Ian's head was not increasing, so a shunt would not be necessary. Ian's heart condition was getting worse, though, so he was sent to Children's Hospital in Birmingham for catheterization and possible surgery. When they were about to start the procedure, they found that it wasn't necessary. **Another miracle?** We took Ian home and he was kept under close observation.

On March 14th of 1970 we took Ian to the neurosurgeon and the pediatrician for his scheduled checkups. Everything looked good and they sent him back home with us. That evening and night, Ian kept grunting like he was struggling against something. It wasn't loud and he wasn't crying, but it did bother us. Something was wrong, but we didn't know what. In my prayers that night I said, "Lord, if you want Ian back, it's all right with me. I can let him go."

The next morning at ten o'clock I got a call from Jo. "Come home right away. Ian has quit breathing." I rushed home, tried artificial respiration, then rushed him to the hospital. When we got there, they confirmed what we dreaded. Ian had died. Three boys gone. Would there ever be more chances for children?

Later, Jo and I talked about what had happened. I confessed to her what I had prayed the night before Ian died, and she said that she had prayed the same thing. We concluded that a merciful and loving God had spared Ian from surgeries and kept him alive until **we could let him go**. Afterward I noticed that my bitterness over the loss of Kenneth was gone. It was as if I released him to God along with Ian. I strongly felt and believed that Ian's gift to us was to heal us from the loss of Kenneth and to set us free.

Jo and I both believed that God had blessed and sustained us during the trials we experienced with our three boys. They are still very much alive with me today.

13 – Questions (and Answers)

Grief counselors tell us that anger is one of the early stages in the grief process. I think it was sublimated anger that impelled my next step. I wanted to know why. "Why have we lost three children?" "What is this business of life and death all about anyway?" I wanted to know, and I turned to the one source I thought could tell me – the Bible. It suddenly wasn't enough to hear three or four readings in church on Sunday. I had to know more, and soon.

I had started to read the Bible many times in my youth and always started with Genesis. I usually gave up by Leviticus. This time I wanted a revelation, so I started with Revelation. To pave the way I used The Living Bible, a modern, easily understood translation. I didn't get the specific answers I wanted, but I was gaining knowledge of God. Jo helped me in my search by turning on Billy Graham whenever he was on TV, and discussing my readings with me. She had a superior knowledge of scripture, salvation, and Christian life, but she never acted superior. She was not preachy and she was gentle. She knew how deficient my faith was, but never belittled me. Much later I would proudly say of Jo, "She would, 'not break a bruised reed or quench a smoldering wick.'" (*Matthew 12:20, RSV*)

Spring break in 1970 came just two weeks after Ian's death, and we felt that it would be good for us to take advantage of Jen's time off from school and get away as a family. We went to Mother and Dad's place in Dade City and used that as a base for exploring Tarpon Springs, Clearwater, St. Petersburg, and Tampa. We boarded Kitty at our vet's while we were gone. On returning home, we learned she had gotten away from her handler one day and broken a bottle of insecticide concentrate. She was doused with the liquid and the vet was not able to save her. Her loss was very hard for us to take, especially so soon after Ian's death. Dr. Walker offered us a cat he called Crinkle Ear because of a deformed ear, but we weren't ready to adopt another cat so soon. In May we got Emily, a lovely long-haired, black and white kitten.

The Boeing Company sent me to Mt. Kisco, New York in August of '70 to supervise component qualification tests at one of our suppliers. I asked Ward Gately, the headmaster of Evangel, if Jen could start school late. He said, "She'll probably learn more there than she will in school," and willingly gave permission. So, I was able to take Jo and Jen with me. The test program lasted three weeks, which gave us time to see all the sights in New York City. We had a grand time, which helped us get through our grief.

Shortly after we returned, Jo found out from Paige Owen, one of her collie friends, about a thirty-acre farm for sale in Limestone County. There were twenty acres under cultivation and ten acres of mature trees with a spring and a stream, Mason Woodfin Creek. Some of the local people thought it was overpriced at ten thousand, but we didn't. We loved it and bought it. There wasn't a house on the property, but that was fine, because we wanted to design and build our own. We knew we would probably never use the property in Canada, so we sold it to pay for the farm and got ten times as much as I originally paid for it.

In November Emily was nearly full grown. We left her outside while we went to a day-long fiddler's convention, but when we returned home that night, she wasn't there, didn't come home, and we never found her.

Jo had started the fall of 1970 by showing Sheila in a Huntsville match and winning a blue ribbon. Then she bred Sheila to Star, one of Betty Hamilton's dogs. Sheila had her first litter of pups in December of 1970. We kept a male from the litter and named him Hercules. At the same time, we had Buttons, a kitten with spots like an ocelot. Buttons had been raised with dogs and she used to bark at us. She would sit on her scratching post, look down at the pups in the whelping box, and bark like a dog. Unfortunately, Buttons also disappeared.

Jo had Sheila bred again, to Oro, a dog belonging to Anne Cross, a friend in Chattanooga. Sheila had her second litter of pups in August of 1971. Jo started showing two of the pups, Annie and Spanish Gold, when they were three months old. Jenifer trained as a junior handler and joined her mother in showing the dogs. Jo sold all of the pups from Sheila's second litter except Annie, who she kept for future showing and possible breeding. Jenifer and Jo both won several trophies.

Jenifer had been asking for a Siamese cat. In January of 1971 Paige offered Jen one of her purebred kittens. Jenifer picked out a lavender point male. Jo helped her decide on the name Ming. In June of that same year we got a brown tabby female kitten we named Cricket.

The next winter Cricket met up with a white angora cat and had a litter of three kittens. One was stillborn, another died at birth, and the third, a lovely white "Cotton" ball, had paralysis of the hindquarters. Cotton was having a lot of trouble, and there was no way of helping her, so we reluctantly had her put to sleep. In July of 1972 Cricket had a second litter of kittens. We kept a long-haired, gray and white one we named Phyllis.

One day in the early fall Cricket brought home a young bird in her mouth, with another young bird following. Because of their markings, I thought they were baby quail. Jo said flatly, "They're chickens."

"No, they're quail; look at the markings. One is female the other male."

"No! They're chickens."

I took them way out in the field, hoping their mama would find them, but they came right back. After several such attempts we decided to keep them. They grew into a lovely black hen and multi-colored rooster. Jenifer had a lot of fun showing our rooster in a family pet show, where she tried to win a ribbon for most unusual pet. Our home turned into a zoo that was the delight of the neighborhood children.

Apollo 15 blasted off from Cape Kennedy on July 26, 1971, carrying LRV-1. It was quite a thrill for me to be at one of the control consoles supporting the mission. LRV engineering work was complete, so from then on I was assigned to support the building, testing, and flights of LRV-2 and LRV-3 as needed. The major portion of my work became involved with company-sponsored projects.

Apollo 16 (LRV-2) flew on April 16th, 1972. The mission was so successful that I was only put on call for Apollo 17 (LRV-3). Apollo 17 flew on December 7th, 1972, and that marked the end of Boeing's involvement with the space program. After Apollo 17, there was no follow-on spacecraft work for Boeing, and they began to look for other endeavours to maintain the Huntsville facility.

One of my first post-Apollo projects was designing and developing an automated telephone system; it was cutting edge technology then. A main feature would be caller ID. I was assigned to the Electronics Testing Laboratory, working for Bill, a man I judged to be a hardheaded, loud-talking Pole. There was keen interest in the telephone project, and a lot of job-concerned individuals bombarded me with suggestions and criticisms, trying to influence the design and work. I was not the nicest person to deal with in those days; I resented any demands that interfered with my work, and made my resentments known. However, there was something else going on inside me. As the space program slowed down, I had more time for Bible study and spiritual growth. In the midst of all the work-related conflicts, I developed a dislike for myself as a person. I could not reconcile my behaviour with how I thought a Christian should act.

14 – Born Again

One night while on my knees in prayer, I told Jesus, "I am sick of my life the way it is. I am tired of trying to live it on my own. Please, Dear Jesus, come into my life and live it for me." Thanks to Billy Graham, I knew what was wrong and I had learned from him how to pray for the remedy. Jesus came into my life, as he promised (*Revelation 3:20*), and I found myself changing.

When I told Jo about my surrender to Jesus she said, "Thank heaven! I have about worn out my knees praying for you these past fifteen years." I thanked Jo for her prayers and marveled at her wisdom and patience.

After this turning point I began a practice of praying on my knees every night at about nine-thirty, for an hour to an hour-and-a-half before going to bed. Most of that time I spent listening to God. A slow, gentle review of my past began, along with day-to-day guidance. I was experiencing something like the fourth step in Alcoholics Anonymous, the Moral Inventory. Over a period of weeks, things I had repressed or forgotten were brought to mind, one by one. Some of it was hard to take; we tend to repress those things that cause shame or pain. I confessed past sins and asked to be forgiven. I acknowledged past hurts and asked for healing of the memories. I tried to make restitution for money I had stolen in my early teen years, but could not locate the people. To make up for it, I gave the money to a Christ-centered drug rehabilitation program.

Also, I felt the need to make peace with people I had quarreled with. One of those people was Bill. I was leaving work one night and Bill was alone in his office. I hesitated about going in to see him. What good would it do? But I was prompted by God to do it, regardless of the outcome. "Bill, may I talk to you for a moment?"

"Yes, come on in."

"I want to apologize for being so quarrelsome with you and constantly disputing your authority."

Being the rather tough guy that he was, Bill said, "Oh, I didn't notice. To me it was just part of getting the job done. Tell me, what brought this about?" I told Bill about my surrender to Jesus. He said that was interesting, and shared some of his faith with me. I found him to be a man of deep faith and much love. Then he said, "Did you go over to the Personnel office today?"

"No."

"Did anyone contact you from Personnel?"

"No."

"H-mmm, that is interesting, because they were supposed to call you in to tell you that you were being promoted to Specialist Engineer, with a hefty raise. And you didn't know about it?"

"No."

I thanked God that He had led me to talk to Bill that night; I'm sure my apology would have meant nothing had I known about the promotion beforehand. I wondered why Personnel had not contacted me. **Was this God at work?** I found in Bill a new Christian friend. This was just the beginning.

The focus of my life changed. I spent more time listening to church services than classical music. I especially liked listening to the First Baptist Church while I was getting ready to go to church at Nativity. I liked many of the Baptist hymns; they seemed to be more personal, spirited, and place more emphasis on salvation. I gave serious thought to joining First Baptist, until one Sunday when the minister preached a blistering sermon on tithing. If you were going to be a member of that church, you had to tithe. I gave more to the church than most members, but I wasn't ready to commit 10% of my gross pay. I shared this with Jo and she seemed a little shocked. "You mean you haven't been tithing?" Her spiritual depth would not let her consider anything less. I had been increasing my pledges, but just couldn't go to a full tithe right away. Yet, I still desired a freer worship. I made up my mind; I would go to Fr. Joffrion and ask him to let us use the parish hall on Sunday evenings to sing some good old gospel hymns.

At church the next Sunday I resolved to talk to Fr. Joffrion, but he announced, "We are going to have a Faith Alive weekend." Outside visitors would witness to us of their faith in Jesus, and there would be lots of evangelical music. I set my plan aside.

15 – The Wind Blows Where it Will *(John 3:8)*

To prepare for the Faith Alive weekend, members of Faith Alive conducted meetings with our church members. One lady from Montgomery, Louise Mohr, gave a dynamic talk about the power of Christ in her life. Louise told us about being baptized by immersion as an adult. This rang a bell with me; several people I worked with had questioned the validity of my infant baptism, and told me that I needed to be baptized as an adult by immersion. This bothered me greatly, because I wanted to get right with God as much as possible, but had never before doubted my baptism. When Louise finished her talk, she asked for questions. I asked her to tell us more about her baptism. She began by telling us about baptism in the Holy Spirit, namely the Pentecostal, or Charismatic, experience. She asked me, "Have you been baptized in the Holy Spirit?"

"Well, I received the Holy Spirit when I was confirmed."

"Do you speak in tongues?"

"No, and I hope I never do."

I certainly did not want to experience anything beyond my comprehension or control. Those words would come back to haunt me later.

I made a note of all the Bible references that Louise gave, went home that night, checked them out, and found that everything Louise said was right. Was I missing something? I concluded that God had taken what I did understand, the water baptism, to lead me to something that I didn't understand, the baptism of the Holy Spirit. I thought, ***"How neat of God!"***

Jo and I attended the weekend. It was great. It was what I was looking for. The program emphasized having a personal relationship with Jesus Christ. The team members told how they experienced coming into and developing a relationship with Christ, and how their lives had been changed. We spent a lot of time singing revival-style hymns. The team led small groups in individual homes for sharing and prayer. After the weekend, we organized small group meetings in homes, and had larger meetings at the church for all the Faith Alive attendees.

I met John Nicely at one of the church meetings. John is fifteen years younger than me and about the opposite in personality. John was an optimist. I wasn't. John warmed up to me, though, and asked, "Have you read <u>Nine O'clock in the Morning</u> by Dennis Bennett?"

"No, I haven't."

"You should get it. It's powerful."

The book told the story of Dennis Bennett, an Episcopal priest, and how he developed a Charismatic church in Seattle. I got the book. John was right about its power. I wanted more.

When the small group meetings came to an end, John, his wife Mary, Jo, Jenifer and I started meeting for prayer and praise with other Faith Alive folk on Monday evenings in the chapel at Nativity. People from other churches began to join us; they would see the lights on and come in from the street for prayer. Many healings took place during those Monday meetings. Jo and I grew close to John and Mary, and a kinship developed between us that has lasted to this day. Jo and I became Faith Alive team members and started going to other churches as witnesses and group leaders. Jenifer joined us as a youth team member during the spring of 1973 weekend at Grace Church in Birmingham. While we were there, Phyllis had a litter of kittens at home. We kept one and named her Frances, after Saint Francis. She was part Siamese, and having her helped soften the pain of Jenifer's loss of Ming the previous year, who apparently had been poisoned.

Our Faith Alive activities brought me into contact with people involved in Faith At Work, a non-denominational movement. Faith Alive was patterned after Faith At Work, but tailored for the Episcopal Church. Similar movements formed in the Methodist and Presbyterian churches. Faith At Work was different. They did not go into churches, but held weekend conferences at conference centers around the country. One of the architects of Faith At Work was Fr. Sam Shoemaker, an Episcopal priest and one of the architects of Alcoholics Anonymous.

Many of the people I met from Faith At Work were Charismatic. Ruefully remembering (and regretting) my previous words about the Charismatic experience, I decided to attend a Faith At Work conference and seek baptism in the Holy Spirit. In February of 1973 I went to the conference held in Fort Walton Beach, Florida. What an experience that was!

I left Huntsville in clear weather. Radio weather forecasters were reporting heavy snow in Montgomery. I was skeptical. I knew how Southerners over-reacted to snow. But the forecasters were not exaggerating. Heavy snow was falling and the authorities were closing roads into and out of Montgomery. I got through Montgomery and onto Highway 231 just before it was closed. By then the forecasters were reporting five inches of ice on the roads further south. I found that hard to believe. A half-inch, yes. Five inches? Come on, now!

As I got farther down the road, I learned what five inches of ice was. Ice was coming down in BB-sized pellets and quickly piling up. All I could see was a blanket of ice and I couldn't tell where the road was. I looked at my side mirror and saw something that amazed me. The tires would create a path and then the ice pellets would flow back in and cover it. Thankfully, I got to Fort Walton Beach without mishap.

In the small group meetings, I was involved in some deep ministry to others who had spiritual needs, but I did not get the opportunity to seek baptism in the Holy Spirit. Maybe my earlier words were not going to be set aside. Yet, I felt spiritually nurtured. At our closing meeting I shared the following with the conference attendees: "I came here looking for a specific blessing from God. Instead, God used me to bless others. I thankfully learned that I could not set the agenda for God's work." I was so thoroughly blessed by this conference, I resolved to take Jo to the next one in our area."

16 – The Call

The next Faith At Work conference was in April of 1973, in Gatlinburg, Tennessee. I thought, "How wonderful to be able to take Jo and also experience spring in the Smoky Mountains!" I was not looking for anything for myself at this conference, I only wanted Jo to experience it. **God had some surprises for us.**

The conference was for adults only, so Jenifer spent the weekend with a friend.

Along with plenary sessions, the conference had workshops and small group meetings. At my small group meeting on Friday night we were discussing ministry, and I told our group, "I think the ordained ministry is as obsolete as the dodo bird. The real ministry of the church resides with the laity." I didn't know it, but our group leader was a Presbyterian minister.

After the Saturday morning workshops, Jo enthusiastically told me about the leader of the healing workshop she attended, an older man who left his occupation as a sales representative to attend Lexington Seminary and become a priest. She remembered Fr. Smith's encouraging me to consider ordination, and saw this as a possibility for me. I heard her, but really didn't consider the possibility. That afternoon I went to the spirituality workshop. Part of the workshop involved quiet prayer and meditation. During one of the silent periods, I heard a voice in my mind that said, "I want you in a healing ministry."

For some reason I wasn't surprised, and I just silently replied, "Ordained?"

"Yes."

That was all. I felt like I had been kicked in the stomach by a mule. This was real. I couldn't lightly dismiss this experience.

The discussion question that night in our small group meeting was, "If you could do something different than your present occupation, what would you like to do?" Everyone except me spoke to the question, and all said they were really quite satisfied with what they were doing. As the meeting closed and started breaking up, someone said, "Hey, we haven't heard anything from Dick."

Everybody went back in and sat down and the leader put the question to me. I said, "I would be an Episcopal priest." You could have heard a pin drop on that hotel room's carpet. They all remembered what I had said the night before.

Jo and I talked about what happened, but did not come to any conclusion. We went to bed and I fell asleep rather quickly. Later I awoke to see a figure about six feet tall, clothed in a friar's robe and hood, standing at the foot of the bed. For some reason, I was not startled by the apparition, but was at ease, although filled with wonder. The room was absolutely dark, but a soft, dim light surrounded the figure. I could not see the face, but my instinct told me it was Jesus. In my mind I could hear him say, "If you cannot answer the call, it is alright."

"Lord," I said, "Do you want me to answer the call?"

"If you cannot answer the call, it is alright."

I felt greatly at peace, and greatly relieved that "the call" was not a do or else die proposition.

Jo and I had a lot to talk about on our way home the next day. I believed that I had received a definite call, and she believed the call had been made known to her through her own experiences at the conference. Interestingly enough, several people had asked us if I was a minister. Now the big question was, "What are we going to do about it?"

During one of my morning-prayer-with-coffee times, I told God, "This idea of me becoming a priest is crazy."

I heard in my mind, "Read Psalm 37:4."

Now there was no way in the world I could have known what Psalm 37:4 was. I was not that well read in the Old Testament. I opened my Bible and there I saw it. "Take delight in the Lord and he will give you the desires of your heart." (*RSV*)

I thought about that, and said to myself, "Yes, that has been a desire of my heart."

It had surfaced several times in different ways, but I always said, "It's not possible, just not possible."

The next verse totally inspired and encouraged me. "Commit your way to the Lord, trust in him, and he will act."

We kept quiet about our experience and said nothing to anyone about being called. However, one Sunday our Assistant Rector, Fr. Hoyt Winslett, told me that he thought the Holy Spirit had really grabbed ahold of me.

17 – Living Waters *(John 7:38)*

Many times at prayer, I told the Lord, "I would feel better equipped to answer your call if I was baptized in the Holy Spirit." Nothing happened until Memorial Day, 1973. The weather was great and I had been working in the yard. While my body was occupied, my mind kept dwelling on one thing – baptism in the Holy Spirit. I decided I needed to do something about it. There was a Pentecostal Holiness Church, Faith Chapel, about half a mile away from us. It was about five o'clock in the evening, and I decided to call Joel McGraw, the pastor. Surprise, surprise! He was in the office and he was alone. I asked him, "Can I meet with you?"

"When?"

"This evening."

"Well, yes, but I've been working in the church yard and I'm in a flannel shirt and kind of grimy."

"That's alright, because I'm in the same condition also."

I drove to the church right away. He asked me what I wanted. "I would like you to pray for me to receive baptism in the Holy Spirit."

He looked a little surprised, and said, "Why do you think you should have it?"

I told him of my surrender to Christ and the feeling of being called, and that the Bible told me the Spirit was for all believers. Joel picked up his Bible and read the following to me: "He that believeth on me, as the scripture hath said, out of his belly shall flow rivers of living water. But this spake he of the Spirit which they that believe on him should receive." (*John 7:38-39a, KJV*) Joel had me kneel, placed his hands on my head and began praying for me to receive the Holy Spirit. I had a feeling of something coming over me. I started laughing and slowly fell backwards until I was resting with my back against a bookcase. The laughter continued – not a raucous, loud laughter, but a deep, incessant laughter. Joel praised the Lord repeatedly and thanked Him for answering his prayer. I didn't speak in tongues, but I did feel that something meaningful had happened. After I quieted down, I had a good feeling of tiredness. I thanked Joel, and he invited me to join them anytime for worship. He said that quite a few Episcopalians, Presbyterians, and Methodists attended their services, that I wouldn't feel out of place. This was the beginning of a long relationship with Joel

McGraw and the Pentecostal churches.

    I went home. I had been gone for an hour, and Jo said, "Gee, I didn't expect to see you so soon. Sometimes those things can last for hours." Again, much to her credit, she, though being raised a Pentecostal, had never pushed her religion on me or displayed a sense of superior knowledge. She strongly believed that the husband should be the spiritual head of the family, and she trusted in her prayer and in the Lord to act.

    I went to bed a bit disappointed, because the only outward sign I displayed was the laughter. Some time later, while in bed, I do not know for how long, I was talking out loud and woke myself up. Jo and Jen were asleep in their rooms and did not hear me. The words were coming in a steady stream, only they weren't in English. The language sounded to me like it was Polynesian. Wow! It had happened to me. I felt anointed, empowered, and hungry for more.

18 – New Vistas

Our lives were becoming more church oriented after the Faith Alive experience. Jenifer became a regular attendee of summer camp at Camp McDowell, our diocesan church camp. She was confirmed into full church membership on April 1, 1973, and showed an interest in becoming an acolyte, a role previously reserved for boys only. We encouraged her to ask Fr. Winslett to admit her to the acolyte program. He readily accepted and started training her, and she became the first girl acolyte to serve at Nativity. She began as a Torchbearer and rose all the way through the ranks, gaining particular favor as Server, because of her reliability and attention to detail. Several girls from Jenifer's Sunday School class followed her lead and became acolytes also.

Every year in late summer, Huntsville hosted the Northeast Alabama State Fair. In 1973 the Oak Ridge Boys, a gospel quartet, performed as part of the onstage entertainment. Jo had loved gospel music since her childhood, and she had heard the Oak Ridge Boys on the Grand Ole Opry as early as 1945. She and Jen were both fans and had several of their records. Jo seized this opportunity for us to see the group in person. We all went, and loved the Oak Ridge Boys. Jo and Jen met the group after the first show and had a poster and record album signed. They stayed around for the second show, while I went to see the fair's technical exhibits.

After the experience of seeing the Oaks, we began going to live shows much more frequently. We went to concerts in Birmingham, Nashville, and many towns in between, as well as Huntsville, and also saw such fine popular shows as the Black Watch and the Royal Lipizzaner Stallions. Jo took Jenifer and her friends to pop and rock concerts, and we all attended many gospel concerts.

Jo became acquainted with the owners of WNDA, the Christian radio station in Huntsville. She went to work for them as a part-time secretary, and soon became the disc jockey on the station's "Saturday Night Singing" gospel music program. This is how Jenifer described her mother's accomplishments in a magazine article:

> *She became one of the first female disc jockeys in Huntsville, AL, and the first on a commercial FM station, winning awards and quickly securing the prime Saturday*

night show at a time when most woman DJs were relegated to overnight slots or weekday dead zones. While she was still too young for working papers, she got her daughter into the station's disc jockey training program, apprenticing her both behind the scenes and on the air during her own show, and even procured a press pass for her so she could accompany her backstage and to exclusive events. She taught her how to conduct an interview, how to report on a concert or publicity event, and how to have fun doing so.

Jo became well known among the gospel performers and promoters, and was invited to join the Oak Ridge Boys organization in Nashville to do publicity work. Jo declined, and continued her radio work. On June 1st, 1978 Jo was given the "Golden Mike" award by Singing News, the gospel music trade publication.

Jenifer had the same love of and inclination toward music as her mother. She, at various times, has played piano, bass guitar, drums, and keyboards. At the time of this writing she has an online music critique and news publication, Tone and Groove.

Baptism in the Holy Spirit brought a whole new set of activities into our lives. We started going to Prayer and Praise meetings at other churches and greatly expanded our circle of friends. I became enthusiastically involved in a variety of ministry activities, a response common in people with new and profound spiritual experiences. One of the Faith Alive team leaders told me, "They should lock people up for six months after they receive baptism in the Holy Spirit." I can now understand why. My sudden busy-ness took me away from home and family, and sometimes made them feel left out. Fortunately, Jo was familiar with the dynamics and was very patient with me. Sad to say, I was not always sensitive to the needs of my family, and misunderstandings with Jo sometimes arose. Sometimes it meant going to bed late, but we would not skip prayers and we resolved our problems before saying prayers, because of the commitment we made during our pre-marriage counseling sessions.

We had another source of strain within our church. Some of the families at Nativity were of the old Huntsville aristocracy. Not all of those people approved of Faith Alive and the evangelical thrust. Jo was treated with disdain by some of the women. Some of Jenifer's peers were quite snobbish, which caused her a lot of hurt. She couldn't reconcile their behaviour to her concept of Christianity. Jenifer did find a larger faith community through all the friends she made at Camp McDowell. There were a lot of good, friendly people at Nativity, though, and they outweighed the hurtful ones. Interestingly, no one exhibited those negative attitudes toward me.

I still had to deal with the sense of being called to the ordained ministry. I made an appointment with Fr. Joffrion to discuss it with him. I felt pretty comfortable about doing so, because, knowing the church's past attitudes toward divorce, I believed I would be immediately disqualified and that would be that. I told Fr. Joffrion about Jesus speaking to me, and was surprised that he didn't advise me to see a psychiatrist. He paid full attention and gave credence to what I was saying. Then I mentioned the divorce and remarriage situation. Again, surprise. "That would have disqualified you a few years ago, but the church is now more inclined to judge a person on the basis of where they are now." I was not off of the hook. He did tell me about the difficulties involved in going through the ordination process, because of an abundance of clergy and candidates.

I have the sometimes-regrettable tendency to choose the easiest and quickest way to accomplish something, so I decided to visit the small seminary in Lexington, Kentucky. I had a most enjoyable visit with Bishop Moody, the founder and dean. He said he thought I had a valid call to ministry, and that I could enter Lexington Seminary. He said I probably would have no trouble finding part-time employment, and he was sure he could find a bishop who would ordain me. I thought about it. This door was open, and other people were taking this route to become ordained.

But I wasn't comfortable with the situation. The specter of looking for the easy way reared its ugly head. Lexington Seminary had begun as a diocesan school and was not accredited. The other problem was lack of scholarship money through the school. I went back to Huntsville and decided to apply to St. Luke's Seminary at University of the South, Sewanee, Tennessee. Attendance at Sewanee would give me greater credibility. I applied and they called me for an interview. The interview did not go as well as I would have liked. Student members of the entrance committee took exception to my not being in favor of decriminalizing marijuana. The dean noted my Faith Alive activities and said the evangelical zeal of "Faith Alivers" had caused them problems in the past. Jo deplored the condition of seminary housing and stifled her tears all the way home. A short time later I received a letter from Sewanee telling me that my application had been denied. I really wondered: Lexington was still open; Sewanee was closed. I felt I needed to talk to our bishop, The Rt. Rev. Furman C. Stough, before going any further.

I asked Fr. Joffrion to make an appointment for me to meet with Bishop Stough during his next visit to Church of the Nativity. I met with the bishop and he listened seriously to what I had to say. I talked about my experience of being called, told him about the rejection from Sewanee, and that I did not know what I should do. He listened intently, made no comments, then said, "How do you feel about what is happening?"

"I don't know, but I still believe that I am supposed to become a priest."

I was greatly encouraged when he said, "I don't always agree with the decisions of seminary deans. I will be in touch with you soon."

I went home to wait.

About a month later, I got a letter from Bishop Stough asking me to come to a meeting at Carpenter House, the Diocese of Alabama offices in Birmingham. In talking things over at church, I found that John Nicely, George Parker, and Bill Ealy, all members of Nativity, had received the same invitation. The four of us went to Carpenter House together. The Bishop's secretary ushered us into a large conference room. We were all quite surprised to see nearly fifty people there. The Bishop began by saying, "Look around you. There are forty-three of you here, all believing that you have been called to the ordained ministry. The problem is we only have an average of three openings a year, and my policy has been to not ordain a person unless I can give him a position." He then sought our comments and opinions. One ameliorating factor was that some of the men were seeking ordination as non-stipendiary deacons only, but there was still the bulk of us to deal with. Bishop Stough said he wanted us to test our vocations by enrolling in the Education for Ministry (EFM) program from the seminary at University of the South, and engaging in supervised ministry in our local churches.

I enrolled in EFM and was appointed to the Missions Committee at church. One of my first tasks was to investigate a newly opened rescue mission downtown. I was so impressed with the work of The

Downtown Rescue Mission, that I became active in their ministry. During the next two years I conducted chapel services, was licensed by the mission as a Minister of the Gospel, and became president of the board of directors. In addition, I made pastoral calls under the supervision of Fr. Joffrion.

Meanwhile, Richard left San Francisco in early 1973 and returned home to Ferndale, Michigan. He married Marilyn Burns in October. Richard had known Marilyn years before, through family ties, when she was a child. His perception of her had changed since she had become a young lady. Richard and Marilyn had a daughter, Erin Kathleen, born on November 10, 1975.

By 1974 Jo and Jenifer had become more involved with gospel music and Christian radio. Jo's mother and dad moved to Harvest, a little farming town north of Huntsville, and they joined us in our church and gospel music adventures.

One evening, Jo, Jenifer, Gran, Gramper and I went to Faith Chapel to hear a gospel group, the Kolenda's. We could hear violent storms during the prayers following the concert. As we were leaving, Fred Wells, the owner of WNDA and a deacon of Faith Chapel, told us, "When you get out, turn your radio on and thank God you were safe here tonight."

Power was out all over the county. It was the Night of the Twisters, April 3, 1974. Tornadoes had hit many parts of the South and Midwest, including southwest Huntsville and the Harvest area. Gran and Gramper stayed with us for the night, and we set up our camp stove and lanterns.

We took Gran and Gramper home the next morning. The destruction was terrible. We had to move debris to get through on their street. Gran's house was still standing, but the front porch and carport columns were damaged, and the house had shifted about an inch on its foundation. The house just south of them had broken windows. The rest of the houses south of them were gone; only the foundations remained. Thankfully, only one woman was injured, and all of the neighborhood animals survived. The next day John Nicely and I loaded my pickup truck with chainsaw, axes and gasoline. We went into areas that were hard hit and worked to clear away downed trees and wreckage. Jo and Jen made sandwiches and took them to the overworked DJ's operating WNDA radio with generators.

A year later a smaller tornado hit our neighborhood. It was a warm spring day and we spent most of it working outside. We were relaxing and eating popcorn in the dinette at ten o'clock that night when the storm started. The wind came up quickly and very strong. Jenifer said, "Daddy, I'm scared."

I was about to say, "There's nothing to be afraid of," when I saw the patio doors bow in and look like they were going to break loose.

"I'm scared, too."

Then it sounded like a freight train going over the house. There was little time to pray, except to thank God that we were still safe after the noise stopped. I looked out the patio door and saw a big branch on the doorstep. We looked outside. Our sixty-five-year-old cherry tree was uprooted, and a massive cedar was snapped off. The cedar tree toppled the chickens' house and collapsed Jenifer's old swing set. Somehow the chickens escaped unharmed. The high winds and driving rain tore shingles off one corner of the roof, and eroded the mortar between the bricks on the chimney. Large branches from the cherry tree had collapsed the brick wall on the patio, damaged a corner of the roof, and fallen on and in the dog pens. Fortunately, we had procrastinated and not put Sheila and Annie in their pens. When the tree roots heaved up, they raised the bottom of the fence. Sheila stayed in the yard and survived unhurt, but Annie got out through the opening. We called for her frantically, and didn't know whether she had been blown away, or hurt, or what. We were greatly relieved when she returned home later, uninjured. Nine weeks later, Annie presented us with a litter of half German shepherd pups. Fortunately, we found homes for the pups through the people of WNDA.

We were truly blessed. The center of the tornado's path missed our house. Some of our neighbors suffered broken windows and roof damage. Even though it was exciting and left us with a lot of cleanup, it was nothing like the 1974 tornadoes. There were no casualties and house damages were minor.

During 1973 and '74 my work with Boeing required several trips to Seattle. During the evenings I visited St. Luke's, Dennis Bennett's home church, to experience firsthand their worship and ministry. One evening I called home and told Jenifer I would be going to St. Luke's for the Praise and Prayer meeting. She said, "Please have them pray for Cricket to come home. She's been gone all day, we haven't been able to find her, and we're having bad storms."

I said, "Okay."

During that part of the meeting when the ministers prayed for people, I remembered my commitment to Jenifer, and sheepishly asked them to pray for our cat. The way they prayed, you would have thought that Cricket was the most important animal in the world.

After the meeting I went back to the motel and called home. Jo told me that Cricket had come home soaking wet from the storm. I asked, "What time did she come home?"

"Ten thirty."

"How interesting! We prayed for her at eight-thirty, which would have been ten-thirty your time."

Through other church acquaintances, I had the blessed opportunity to spend a renewal weekend at Church of the Redeemer in Houston, Texas. Redeemer was another powerful Charismatic church. The members lived in community with one another near the church and provided various ministries to the poor in their neighborhood.

Like many spirit filled people from other churches, I regularly attended the Wednesday night and Sunday night services at Faith Chapel. Then I progressed to a point where I started going to Sunday school at Faith Chapel and then to Nativity for the eleven-fifteen Sunday morning service. This seemingly divided loyalty began to bother me and I prayed for guidance. In that silent voice of my mind, the Lord told me, "Fr. Joffrion is your pastor, Joel McGraw is your teacher." This dispelled any doubts I had about direction; I was in Faith Chapel to learn and experience "body" ministry (ministry by all of the members one to the other, and to the community).

By mid 1974 my work at Boeing came to a close. They asked me to transfer to Seattle. I felt that if I went to Seattle I would have to set aside my efforts toward ordination and start all over again there. Also, Jo did not want to go to Seattle, so I turned the transfer offer down. At the time, two companies wanted to employ me as a consultant, so I wasn't really worried. But 1974 was a bad year economically and I learned a hard lesson about the consulting business. A lot of consulting activity is directed toward capital expansion. When the economy tightens, expansion is suspended and consultants are not needed anymore. In a matter of two months I joined the ranks of the unemployed and was on the open job market.

By November of 1974 I gained employment as a senior engineer for Avco, a commercial electronics company. The pay was considerably less than what I made at Boeing, but it was a job. Having a nongovernment job gave me the luxury of a straight forty-hour workweek, which provided us with a lot of freedom to pursue our church activities, gospel music, concerts, and Christian radio. Our cup was overflowing. Jo had her work at the radio station and Jenifer was working along with her. I had EFM and church work, and we all went to gospel singings within a hundred miles, following groups we liked. We also entertained one of the out of town groups at Gran and Gramper's house.

    1975 was a big year for Jenifer. She went into the ninth grade at J. O. Johnson High School, a big public high school a quarter-mile away from our house across an open field. Although Evangel had an excellent elementary school, their high school was small and offered very few courses. Jenifer asked to leave Evangel and go to Johnson. Her main interests were art and writing, and Evangel did not have much to offer in those fields. Jenifer blossomed at Johnson; they had excellent writing and art teachers and the school was large enough to offer a good curriculum and good extracurricular activities. Apparently Jen's interest in creative writing was contagious, because it sparked the same interest in Jo.

    In 1976 we loaded up our turquoise and white '72 Dodge pickup with the camper top, and set out for Banff, Alberta. We met my parents and our two young nieces there on July 29th and celebrated my birthday. It was a fabulous trip. We went up through the Northwest, saw mountains and glaciers, and returned through the Southwest and saw the desert regions.

    After our return in early August, Northrop offered me a job working on the Space Shuttle, along with a fair increase in pay. In September of 1977 Northrop merged their efforts with McDonnell Douglas, and I was faced with layoff or a job under poor working conditions. I took the layoff and immediately found employment with United Space Boosters, working on the Space Shuttle's solid rocket booster.

    We felt doubly blessed; we had a good full life and ***God had always provided*** us with a job when we needed it. I started teaching junior high Sunday School at Nativity, and teaching a science class for GED test candidates at the community center. Jo, Jenifer and I joined the choir at Nativity, one of the best things we ever did. Our choir director, Dr. D. Royce Boyer, was head of the music department at University of Alabama in Huntsville, and he arranged concerts for the choir at the Von Braun Civic Center, accompanied by the Huntsville

Symphony Orchestra, and at other churches, which provided us with wonderful singing experiences.

19 – The Call Takes Shape

My application for postulancy, the first step toward ordination, was beginning to bear fruit. Bishop Stough sent me a list of subjects he wanted me to write about, including a detailed spiritual autobiography. Immediately after Labor Day of 1977 Bishop Stough requested that Jo and I attend BACAM, the Bishop's Advisory Committee on Aspirants to the Ministry, a weekend of intensive interviews at Camp McDowell.

Eight aspirants attended, and we were all very conscious of what Bishop Stough had said about only having an average of three openings a year. Each aspirant had to give a spoken account of how he or she saw themself as a minister. The other seven all sounded eminently qualified and motivated. It was remarkable that there was no feeling of competition between us; it was more like we were all faced with the same challenge and this drew us close together in a very short period of time. We whiled away the time with lively games of Spoons while the committee members conferred and made their judgments.

The bishop called us together and gave us the committee's recommendations. All of us were accepted as postulants, and only two would have their seminary start date delayed a year because of family or school considerations. The sad part was the rest of us had to wait until 1978 to start seminary, because admissions had closed for the year. Jo and I were surprised that Bishop Stough did not want us to wait until 1979, to allow Jenifer to finish high school first. After more than four years of going through the process we were finally on our way, and we were very glad we had done things in the conventional manner.

We were occupied with applying for seminary during the rest of 1977. Bishop Stough asked me to apply at Episcopal Theological Seminary of the Southwest in Austin, Texas. I went for the interview, was well impressed with the school and faculty, but still wanted to go to Sewanee. To forestall any decision by Seminary of the Southwest before I could have another interview at Sewanee, I delayed sending them my transcripts. But, they went ahead and accepted me in November on the strengths of my Graduate Record Examinations.

Jo and I went to Sewanee again and had a much more congenial and satisfactory interview, but Jo said, "You're wasting your time. We're going to Texas." Shortly thereafter, the dean at Sewanee called me and said they were withholding approval of my application. He suggested that since I was already accepted at Seminary of the Southwest, I should go there. I called Bishop Stough.

"Bishop Stough, I just got a call from the dean at Sewanee."

"Yes, I know all about it. We had talked the matter over."

"Oh."

I told Jo about the call and the outcome. Her response was quite candid. "I told you that you were going to Texas, Booby."

Along with all the effort needed to make the move, we had to contend with the layoff at Northrop, but **we were blessed** that I was hired by United Space Boosters, which would tide us over until we left for seminary in August.

Then we got a once-in-a-lifetime opportunity. The Nativity choir was going on a two-week concert tour of England and Wales, singing in churches and cathedrals. We signed up and drew our last $3,000 out of the credit union to pay for the trip. We trusted God that we would sell our house in time and be able to pay for our move. We put our house on the market, packed our bags, and set off for England. We gave our real estate agent an itinerary and asked her to let us know if the house sold. At every hotel, we went to the desk and asked, "Are there any messages for us?" The answer was always the same – there were none.

We returned home during the first week of July feeling rather perplexed. My classes would start on August 15th. We were running short of time. July and early August went by and we still did not have a buyer for the house. We worried that we would have to rent a place in Austin until our house was sold.

On the afternoon of the day before we planned to leave Huntsville, our agent came to us with an offer. We decided it was acceptable, but closing would take time, because the buyers were getting a VA mortgage. *Miracle*: we had a bona fide offer in our hands.

We went to Austin, contacted a really dynamic real estate agent there, and started looking at houses. After two days of looking, we settled on one house, but the deal failed, because the seller would not let us assume his mortgage and there was no way that we could finance it ourselves. We went back to the house where we were staying and called the dean to see if we could rent housing at the seminary. *Miracle:* At two-thirty in the afternoon of our last day in Austin, the real estate agent called and said a new listing had just come on the market. We rushed to see it. It was a lovely three bedroom, two bath, four-year-old, stone ranch house in a very good neighborhood. It was a loan assumption, and we could rent it from the owners until our house sale closed. We went back to Huntsville feeling truly blessed. My mother let us cash in some of her own savings bonds for the money we needed to move. This experience caused us to jokingly say, "We have a last minute God." But it also taught us to trust.

    Our move to Austin was quite an operation. We left Sheila with Gran and Gramper, along with our boat. We couldn't keep Brewster, our rooster, because he was so mean, but Gramper knew of a farmer who raised chickens and needed a rooster. He was really pleased to get Brewster. We put Annie and Chick-Chick into dog crates in the camper shell of the Dodge pickup, and the cats into carriers. What a caravan! I was in the pickup with Frances on the seat. Jo and Jen were in the Dodge Monaco with all of our houseplants and Cricket. I guess it's a tabby thing, but Cricket nearly drove Jo and Jen nuts with her caterwauling.

20 – Deep in the Heart of Texas

In mid-August of 1978 it was nothing but hot in Austin. We arrived at our new home in mid-afternoon and felt like we were in the Twilight Zone. There was not a single person anywhere in sight. The tennis courts and swimming pools were empty. Pool water temperatures were 105 degrees and some pools were closed. Our supper that night was cucumber and cream cheese sandwiches, the first of many such suppers.

But when the sun went down, the neighborhood came to life. Adults appeared and children came out to play.

We slept on the floor that first night, and slab floors can be very hard, even with thick carpeting and heavy sleeping bags. The next day, North American Van Lines arrived, and thankfully our stuff was in good condition. There were a few scratches on the furniture, but North American took care of them within a week.

I started the two-week orientation period, and Jo and Jenifer started looking for jobs. Jo thought she would be able to get a position at KLBJ radio, but problems in the Johnson family caused a suspension of new hires. Jo had to start from scratch to find a job. Her only recent work experience was five years at WNDA. Jenifer got the first job in the family, as a clerk in the record department at the nearby Woolco department store. I picked her up after her first day of work and stopped at a pizza parlor on the way home. "Daddy, are we going to get a pizza?"

"Yes, we are. I have a little bit of money left."

"Oh, wow, great!"

There was now going to be something more to eat than cucumber sandwiches.

When I went to the Finance Office at school to arrange for my support, they said we first needed to apply for outside scholarship aid, then know what Jo's income would be and how much support we could get from the Diocese of Alabama. The Diocese said they needed to know what Jo's income would be; their support was conditional upon her working. Well, at least Jenifer had some money coming in, but we were still a month away from closing on our house in Huntsville.

Miracles: Within ten days Jo had a job with State Farm Insurance Co., and their office was less than three miles from our house. We were then able to get commitments of support from the Diocese of Alabama and Church of the Nativity. I took all of our financial data back to the Finance Office. They looked it over and said that they would balance our budget, except they would not allow us to tithe, said it was like "robbing Peter to pay Paul." What we lacked from Jo's salary, my scholarship from Society for the Increase of the Ministry, our church's support, and the diocese's support would be covered by grants from the Joe and Jessie Crump Memorial Fund, one of the scholarship funds at the seminary. We felt doubly blessed, because they didn't make us sell our farm, which was rented out for cultivation, but let us keep it as a source of income. To accomplish all of this in two weeks was really miraculous. We could not agree with the Finance Office concerning the tithe, so we just decided to take it out of the funds from our house sale.

Our financial situation was resolved when classes started. By the end of September, we had closed on the Huntsville house, closed on the house in Austin, paid my mother back for our moving expenses, and had enough money left over to cover our tithes.

Seminary classes began the second week of September, and I found myself nearly overwhelmed by the amount of reading and writing required. I didn't realize how far behind I was getting until about four weeks into the term, when we were hit with a test in Church History. I had not done the required reading and I was not even fully aware that I had missed the assignment. Depressed, I wondered how I would ever make it through. I was used to reading sixty to two hundred pages an hour of technical material, and here I wasn't able to do more than thirty pages an hour.

In my mail the next day was a note from the interim dean, a man from Georgia. "I was wondering how a Southern boy from Alabama was getting along." I welcomed this as Providence guiding me to the right person to talk to.

I went to see Professor Doremus and said, "I wish I could wish that I wasn't here. Do you know what I mean?" He said he did. I told him my problem. (I think he already knew). He was compassionate and encouraging, and said my situation was by no means unique, that I had entered into a very different and hard way of life. He urged me to hang on and do my best, that in two weeks there would be a week off for reading and that would give me a chance to get caught up. Thank heaven for the reading weeks. I did get caught up and was able to pass all my courses that first term.

An objective of seminary training is "formation of the individual." This usually takes the form of some kind of stress. At Seminary of the Southwest they believed in stressing a person academically. Their goal was to produce highly educated and competent graduates. I think seminary was the hardest three years of my life, but also the best.

Life was interesting and good in Austin. There was excellent shopping, good entertainment, good food, and a reasonable cost of living. The nearby mall had an ice skating rink, and Jenifer's northern-bred parents were able to teach that Southern gal ice-skating. And we found one way to beat the heat – go shopping at midnight. By careful shopping we were able to eat as well on half the money we used to spend for food in Huntsville. There were challenges in living on a seminary budget, but there were also ways to accomplish it, and there was a real sense of satisfaction in being able to do so.

The move to Austin really disrupted Jenifer's life, but she took it with a lot of grace. She really loved Johnson High School, the teachers and the classes, and the close friends she had made there. She received excellent art and creative writing instruction, and now she had to leave in her last year. And then there was Steve. They were very serious about one another, and his sister was one of Jenifer's best friends.

Jenifer went into Sydney Lanier High School in Austin and found herself in a school with little academic challenge for her, and many students with a pickup driving, tobacco chewing lifestyle. When she enrolled, her counselor shook his head and said that with her honor courses and college track courses already completed, "We don't know how to place you."

There was a bright side. Jenifer had enough credits to finish high school in just two quarters and was able to take mostly electives. She finished high school in February and graduated on May 31, 1979. We were very proud of her; she finished tenth in a class of 440, and was a member of National Honor Society.

We had wondered about how we would handle college for Jenifer. She had visited University of the South (Sewanee) six years earlier with her church youth group. She was quite impressed with the school and the surroundings, and decided that was where she wanted to go. She had requested that her SAT scores go to Sewanee. Sewanee recruited her on the basis of her high SAT scores, and put together a very good financial aid package for her. Our costs would be Jenifer's transportation and her incidental expenses. Of added benefit, she would be close to Huntsville, which meant spending school holidays with Gran and Gramper and being close to Steve.

Christmas of 1978 was great. I had passed all of my classes, Steve drove to Austin to spend the holidays with us, and we all spent a lot of time ice-skating.

Only one elective subject was offered during the month of January, and you could skip a January term if you wished. I elected to skip the January, 1979 term. This gave me a chance to catch up on house maintenance and rest up from that difficult first semester.

Regular classes started in February, and things just got harder – more reading, more writing. But I did make it through the second semester all right.

I took Clinical Pastoral Education (CPE) during the summer of 1979 at Austin State Hospital, a mental institution. CPE is supervised and peer critiqued pastoral work. Your peers and the supervisor are very critical and often belittling. I would call it chaplain boot camp. I learned a lot about mental illness, mental health care, and myself. Despite some of the unpleasant group sessions, I felt that I had gained a lot in that setting, and arranged to do my field education there during the coming school year.

In midsummer we saw Jenifer off on a plane to Huntsville. We went back home and sadly contemplated a home with no Jenifer. In late August we went to Huntsville, had a good visit with Gran and Gramper, and moved Jenifer into Sewanee.

The Middle Year was more difficult academically, and we had the added requirement of Field Education, a minimum of six hours plus travel time each week. Thanks to the reading weeks and change of pace during the January term, I was getting through the second year okay.

Everything was going well during the spring of 1980 until mid-April. My parents were getting ready for the annual migration from their Dade City, Florida home to their cottage in Canada. This year was different; Mother had come down with shingles and had gone ahead by plane to Sharon's place in Michigan. Father stayed in Dade City to pack the car, close up the house, and then drive north. He had been plagued with continence problems from surgery a year before, but after six months of therapy he seemed to be over it. The third week of April, Uncle Harold called. "We found your dad wandering around in the backyard. He doesn't know what he is doing and he is thoroughly wet."

"Don't try to do anything with him. Get him to the hospital immediately."

He had suffered a stroke. I called Mother and told her what had happened. She and Sharon left Michigan immediately to go to Dade City. I had a critical week of school left before reading week and told Mother that I would leave Austin on Saturday, May 3rd to see Father and be with them. On May 2nd Mother called and told me that Father had unexpectedly died. I immediately made arrangements at school to be gone until final exams began on the 12th, and left for Florida. I assisted the priest from St. Mary's Church at Father's burial service.

Sharon told me quite a bit about Father's death. He had gotten through the critical first stages of the stroke and was not seriously disabled, except for a recurrence of the incontinence. They had done everything they could at the hospital, and his next step was to go into rehabilitation. He refused. Sharon asked him, "Are you going to get better?"

"No."

"Why not?"

"It's not worth it."

So, the doctors said Father would have to go to a nursing home. He said he wasn't going to go. They said, "You have no choice. We cannot keep you here," and made arrangements for him to leave.

They had Father all packed up to go and an ambulance came to take him to the nursing home. The ambulance driver said, "We can't take this man, he's running a fever."

For some unknown reason, Father had developed a high fever. They re-admitted him to the hospital and he died shortly thereafter. I wondered deeply, " How much does our will determine our state of being?" I went back to school and started my finals. I got through them, but felt like an automaton. My ability to think was minimal. My theology professor wisely insisted that I take an incomplete on my term paper and wait until the end of the next term to finish it.

Father's death and the aftermath had a profound effect on me. In April of 1978, the year we left for seminary, Mother and Dad had stayed with us on their journey to the cottage. While Father was getting into the car to leave, he said, "Well, Junior, I guess I'll never see you again." I shushed him and made light of his remark. I wish now that I had not. That parting is indelibly written in my memory.

During my first year in seminary, Father asked me about

baptism. He was concerned about his spiritual well being. He did not know if he had been baptized as a child, so he had his minister baptize him as an adult. He still wondered if that was sufficient. I told him, "Jesus said, 'This is the will of (Him) who sent me, that I should lose nothing of all that (He) has given me,' (*St. John 6:39, RSV*) and I believe that we are given to Jesus through baptism." Soon after our conversation, Father underwent serious groin surgery. His heart stopped on the operating table, but they were able to resuscitate him. I have always regretted that we did not have a chance afterward to talk about what he experienced.

While going through Father's personal effects, I came across a book on Christian spiritual development that he had been reading. It made me feel good to believe my father had found the Lord. Shortly after his death I had two vivid dreams about him, both of them in color. In the first dream, I went into a room where Father was sitting in an overstuffed chair with his back to me. He said, "Everything is alright," and the dream ended. In the second dream, I met Father at the gate of an institution that had a wrought iron fence with brick pillars and a massive wrought iron gate that was partially open. The place looked like a veteran's hospital that I had seen in Michigan. Father was just outside the gate, looking well tanned and healthy, dressed in gray pajamas and a gray housecoat with pale blue and red vertical stripes. I had a strong impression that he was a patient in a place of cure. I went to him and he hugged me. He held me tight and was lifting me up. I said, "Dad, that is starting to hurt."

He said, "That's what it is like here."

I strongly felt that he was in a process of completion, and I reflected upon a belief that what is not completed in our lives here on Earth is completed in heaven. "Growing from strength to strength." (*The Book of Common Prayer, page 488*) I was greatly encouraged by that dream.

I spent my second summer as a chaplain at St. David's Hospital, working mostly in the oncology and neonatal care sections. I attended several terminal cases and sudden death cases. I was awed by what happened during these experiences, like my care to a black minister with an incurable brain tumor. He knew he was dying, and told me that he wanted to go and be with Jesus, but his family wasn't ready to let him go. His nurse said that it was almost a miracle that he kept on living and was free of pain. On one of my visits with the family, his wife said that she felt like she was ready to say goodbye to her husband. He died that night.

I had not realized so much intense ministry could take place through chaplaincy. I gained additional experience through conducting funeral services for patients who were from out of town or did not have a church relationship. I found this to be very meaningful service and I elected to stay at the hospital for my Field Education assignment the coming school year, as well as serve in our church, assisting the priest with services and occasionally preaching.

I tried to finish my theology term paper during the summer, but had a terrible case of writer's block. I was thankful that my professor had given me until the end of the fall term to complete it. Meanwhile, Jo was doing very well at State Farm and had graduated from doing policy work on a typewriter to using a Vydec word processor. Welcome to the world of computers! It was a mammoth machine, bigger than a desk, nothing like the computers we use today.

Our syllabi for the senior year bowled all of us over. A classmate said he went into deep depression when he saw the requirements. It looked like 50% more reading and writing than in our Middler year, plus the General Ordination Exams were coming in January and we had to prepare for them.

When we got into the work, we found we were far more proficient than we were two years earlier. Also, I believe the workload was designed to prevent any "senior relaxation syndrome."

About midway through the term I had quite a frightening experience. I awoke in the dark of midmorning with both arms pinned to my sides and the feeling of huge arms around my chest squeezing me tighter and tighter. I couldn't manage to cry out, and I was terrified. I felt like I was wrestling with the devil and losing. I remembered the reputed power of the Jesus Prayer, and started saying "Jesus, Jesus, Jesus," over and over. Finally the grasp released and I was free. I felt like some force was trying to bring an end to my seminary work. I recalled how Jacob wrestled with the angel of God. I felt like I had wrestled with a demon.

As graduation time drew near, Bishop Stough had me interview as assistant at Nativity in Huntsville, and as rector of St. Andrew's in Sylacauga. Sylacauga is a small, mid-eastern Alabama cotton mill town, probably most famous for being the home of Jim Nabors (Gomer Pyle on TV). St. Andrew's was also Bishop Stough's first church. I will not forget how blazing hot it was the day Jo and I went for the interview. Naturally, we wanted the job at Nativity and to go back to Huntsville.

Days later Bishop Stough called and said, "I've made a decision that will affect the rest of your life. I want you to go to Sylacauga." I looked upon the assignment as being God's will and an opportunity for us. I had long felt that small churches suffered, because they usually had a different minister every two or three years. We didn't want to do a lot of moving, so we went with the expectation of staying and growing. There was no question of a difference in salaries. All newly ordained ministers were paid the same amount. We put our house on the market and made arrangements to move. St. Andrew's had a rectory, so there was no problem finding a place to live.

Graduation came on the 26th of May, 1981, and I received the degree Master of Divinity. How absolutely awesome! I had set out to get a Master's (of Science) degree in 1961 and now, twenty years later, I had achieved that goal. Though the degrees were different, I believe I had the degree God intended for me, rather than the one I thought I wanted. Jenifer was home from school, Mother flew in from Florida for the graduation, the State Farm folks threw a going away party for Jo, and we had a great time. We were very sorry that Jo's mother and dad could not be with us for that happy occasion.

Miracles were still happening. The housing market was getting really tight because of increasing interest rates, but we got a buyer for our house at our asking price, within three weeks. We realized a gain of ten thousand dollars on the sale, much more than we had spent from savings to cover our tithe. I wondered – **what would have happened if we had not tithed during our time in seminary?**

21 – Church Ministry Begins

After graduation we went to Huntsville for my ordination. On the 12th of June, 1981 at Church of the Nativity, Bishop Stough ordained me Deacon. It was a wonderful occasion. The choir performed special music for the service. Fr. Bob Redmon, the rector of St. John's, our church in Austin, preached the sermon. The Episcopal Church Women prepared a sumptuous banquet. Many family members and clergy from out of town came. After the services we went to Fr. Emile and Martha Joffrion's house for a champagne toast.

The next day Gran and Gramper hosted a family reunion at their house. Mother was there, along with Richard, Marilyn and Erin. Sharon, her husband, John Cline, and two of their four children, Joel and Evan, were there also, as well as Aunt Winnifred and Uncle Bill Taylor, and Fr. Bob Redmon.

After a short vacation we left for Sylacauga. We were reduced in numbers, though. Cricket had run away our first month in Austin, Chick-Chick died the first winter, and Annie died a week before graduation. Sheila died the week before we moved back. It was a sad homecoming in some respects, but we still had Frances. She had been my constant companion all through seminary. She would curl up in my lap while I read, and lie on the desk next to me while I wrote.

Our ministry at St. Andrew's started on July 1st. Moving to a small town like Sylacauga was culture shock in many ways. For example, we enjoyed the benefits of the old tradition of "pounding," especially since five of those pounds were tenderloin of beef! But then there was the Pastor of the First Methodist Church, who didn't think the Rector of the Episcopal Church should be seen driving a pickup truck. A Baptist woman told our secretary, Peggy, "I just saw your new preacher driving a pickup truck."

Peggy replied, "That's all right, they're from Texas."

"Oh. That explains that."

It also took awhile to get used to the townspeople asking any stranger, "What church do you go to?" when first introduced.

We were not able to settle into the rectory because of our tax situation. Having made a considerable profit on the sale of our houses, we were subject to a hefty tax if we did not buy a house of equal value to the one we sold in Austin. The church had been renting the rectory before our arrival, and agreed to rent the rectory again and give us a housing allowance. So, we started looking, even though it was a seller's market with mortgage rates at 12% and rising. We looked at all the available houses that we could afford, and found only one that was satisfactory, and it needed a lot of fixing up. When we had resigned ourselves to making an offer on that house, our real estate agent showed up with plans for a lovely Southern style ranch house, and said the builder had a half-acre wooded lot to build it on. We looked at the lot and loved it. It was on the edge of town, in a hilly area, and was so grown up with trees and bushes that we couldn't even get in to see it all. It was like a dream come true. When we closed, the interest rates had gone to 15%, but that did not hinder us, because the market was becoming a buyer's market and the builder had lowered his asking price.

    The second half of 1981 was as eventful as the first half. I plunged into my work wholeheartedly, conducting Morning Prayer services at the church four days a week, in addition to Sunday services. We had a lot of visitors, due to increased employment at the Kimberly-Clark paper mill in Childersburg, a city just ten miles from Sylacauga, and I made it a practice to visit every newcomer. The church was growing so much that they decided not to rent the rectory, but keep it as an office and Sunday School building.

    Then tragedy struck. Our organist suffered a brain hemorrhage, and died right after she got to the hospital. She had grown up in St. Andrew's and was totally committed to the church and church music. We struggled to sing a capella until a fifteen-year-old member, Lisa Coleman, expanded her piano training to include learning the organ.

    The Church required a person to have at least six months of service as a deacon before being ordained to the priesthood. On December 15th I was ordained Priest by Bishop Stough in the Cathedral Church of the Advent in Birmingham. I celebrated my first Holy Eucharist at the Midnight Mass on Christmas Eve.

22 – Family Changes

Jenifer gave us a surprise right after our move to Sylacauga. She and Steve had broken up during her first year at Sewanee. Jenifer and another "preacher's kid," Larry Grover, became good friends during her second year, and then became very serious friends during her third year. Larry was due to graduate in 1982 and had a full scholarship to Princeton for graduate work. They planned to marry once Larry was established in Princeton.

During the Christmas holidays of 1981, Jenifer went with Larry to visit his parents, Charles and Joan Grover, in Syracuse, New York, and then she brought him "home" to meet us. The visit with Larry was a real adventure. A bad snowstorm turned into an ice storm, and it took us five hours to make the 50-mile trip from the airport in Birmingham to our house. Midway, I had to spread sand on the road to get up an incline. The car was shrouded with half an inch of solid ice. We finally made it home, and forty-five minutes later our power went out and stayed out for over a week. There we were, with a stranger in the house, only a fireplace for heat, candles and a Coleman lamp for light, and a camp stove for cooking. It was an interesting time. We were able to get the family room up to 55 degrees. We heated water by the fireplace, cooked on our camp stove, and played a lot of UNO at night to pass the time. Larry was a good sport and a big help through it all. We had not laid in firewood for the winter, so he and I spent our days cutting wood and we all spent our nights burning it.

Another big change came during the spring of 1982. I was driving Mother back north after her winter stay in Florida. A very different mood prevailed on this trip. Mother had put the Dade City house up for sale and was preparing to move in with Sharon, who had just bought a five-bedroom house in Brighton, Michigan. We stopped for the usual midpoint visit at our home in Sylacauga. Mother looked very unhappy at breakfast the next morning. I said, "You look rather unsettled. Is something troubling you?"

"Yes. I really don't want to go live with Sharon, but I don't know what else to do."

"What would you like to do?"

"I'd like to have a little place of my own."

"Do you know where?"

"Yes. Here in Sylacauga."

I told her that I knew the manager of a nice apartment complex. "Would you be interested?"

"Yes."

I set up a meeting with the manager and learned that a newly redecorated apartment would soon be available. That did it for Mother. She paid a deposit and immediately changed her plans.

Later in the summer, the house in Florida sold and Mother moved to Sylacauga. Her stay in the apartment would be short, however. In less than a year's time she bought a small house on a lovely wooded lot on the east side of Sylacauga.

By her third year at Sewanee, Jen had completed all of the art and photography courses she needed for her major except a semester of art history. Required foreign language classes had given her problems, though, and she struggled with math and physics. Her grade point average slipped and she was no longer eligible for a Pell grant. At the end of the '82 school year she fearfully told me that she did not want to go back to school for her Senior year. I listened to her carefully, then told her, "Jen, we asked you to try college for at least two years. We feel like you more than kept your end of the bargain, and you are free to go."

She looked quite surprised and said, "Really?" She was sure old Daddy Bear would kick up a fuss about her not finishing college, and he didn't.

Jenifer spent that summer working as the arts and crafts director at Camp McDowell, and the fall at the NAPA auto parts store as a bookkeeper for Bob Green, one of our church members, and preparing for her wedding. She did get a jolt when her dentist told her she needed to have her wisdom teeth taken out. We decided it was best have it done before she had married and moved away from us.

Along with everything else that was happening in 1982, Jo and I expanded our spiritual lives in the spring by going to Cursillo, an intense weekend of instruction and experience in Christian faith and life. Jenifer went to the next Cursillo, in the fall.

Jenifer and Larry had planned to marry during the summer of 1983. While Jen was working at Camp McDowell, they decided to move the wedding up to December. That left us with four months to plan a wedding on a very tight budget, and get Jenifer's oral surgery accomplished. Jo and Jenifer were able to get a ready-made gown and a custom made veil at reasonable prices. The women of St. Andrew's Church provided the reception, and John Nicely did the photography as a gift.

Jenifer's wedding day was the 18th of December, 1982. It was a gala occasion. Larry's dad, an Episcopal priest, and I jointly performed the ceremony for our children. Jenifer's oldest first cousin, Renée, was Maid of Honor. Larry's older brother, Jim, was his Best Man. All of our families were there, along with John and Mary Nicely from Huntsville, and Dawn Darnell, Jenifer's best friend since the first grade. We had the reception at the church, and dinner at our house for family and visitors afterwards.

Jenifer and Larry took our car for a brief honeymoon, then stayed with us through Christmas and New Year's until it was time for Larry's spring term Larry went back to Princeton to find housing, and Jenifer stayed with us. Larry found an apartment by February, and came back to Sylacauga. He rented a small U-Haul truck, loaded it with Jenifer's furniture, and they set off for New Jersey. In Princeton, Jenifer worked first at Thomas Sweet Chocolates and introduced us to the joys of hand-made chocolate candies. Next, she worked as a cashier at the Superfresh market, and then at Beaky's, a record store.

Larry was awarded a Master of Psychology and Neuroscience degree in 1984. He was awarded the degree Doctor of Philosophy in Psychology and Neuroscience in 1986. Larry continued on at Princeton for a year and a half, doing research and teaching. Jen and Larry then moved to Ravenna, Ohio on the 27th of December, 1987 when Larry received an appointment to North East Ohio Universities College of Medicine.

Except for a two-semester interim at University of Washington in Seattle, Larry did teaching and research at North East Ohio Universities College of Medicine from 1988 to 1993. He is now a full professor, doing teaching and research at Marshall University's College of Medicine in Huntington, West Virginia.

While they were in Ohio, Jenifer continued her education at Kent State University. She took courses in archery, modern poetry, jewelry and metals, and two semesters of poetry workshop, and she assisted in editing, producing, and reorganizing the school's literary magazine. She has become an accomplished artist, photographer, writer, editor, and jewelry crafter.

23 – Life at St. Andrew's

During 1983 the ministry at St. Andrew's continued to grow. Lisa Coleman was doing well as organist and we were able to build up a small, but good choir. Jo and I became certified mentors for Sewanee's off-campus course in theology and ministry, Education for Ministry (EFM), and we soon had a lively EFM group in the church.

In late 1982, the Episcopal Church, the Roman Catholic Church, and the Methodist Church began the Kairos movement in Alabama. Kairos was like Cursillo, except it was for inmates of correctional centers, and all of the proceedings were conducted within the prison walls. I signed up for Kairos #2 in the spring of 1983. Kairos #2 was held at Draper Correctional Center, and that was the beginning of five years of my work in Kairos. After Kairos #1, Bishop Stough, in describing the experience, quoted scripture. "I saw Satan fall like lightning from heaven." (*Luke 10:18, RSV*) The degree and number of conversions were so powerful, those of us on the Kairos teams had that same feeling. In addition to Kairos and EFM, I became a member of the Salvation Army Service Unit and co-founder of Care House, an interfaith welfare center.

During the next three years we saw some growth in the community and the church, and our work and lives continued without remarkable change, but storm clouds were forming overhead. By 1987 we felt the impact of the growing trend to obtain goods and services from foreign countries. Avondale Mills, a long-standing producer of cotton textiles, felt the pressure of foreign competition, and having older, inefficient facilities hampered them from competing effectively. The same thing was happening to Kimberly-Clark, the paper mill in Childersburg. As these two major employers started to shrink, they lost management people, many of whom were the backbone of St. Andrew's. The Coleman's were transferred out of town. That meant we lost our organist, Lisa. We tried to get another organist, without success. Finally, Jo said that she would try to fill the spot. She started taking lessons from a piano and organ teacher in Childersburg. It looked like this was going to be a good solution to our problem, until a self-appointed watchdog over church finances objected to Jo's using the church's organ and utilities for practice. We gave up.

To make up for the loss of members and income, St. Andrew's

joined with Trinity Church in Alpine to share a minister. Trinity was a small church that had been joined with St. Peter's in Talladega. St. Peter's had grown enough that they desired and could afford to separate from Trinity. We were saved economically. It was more work for me, but it was more than worth it. The people of Alpine were great, and Trinity gave us a country facility, which could be used for picnics and retreats.

Not only were we hit in our church and community lives, we were hit in our personal lives. I got a phone call from Marilyn in 1985 telling me that she could no longer tolerate Richard's drinking. There did not seem to be any way of effecting reconciliation, and their divorce soon followed. Richard never remarried. He eventually went into Alcoholics Anonymous and became sober in 1994. He is now a sponsor in his AA group, and is dedicated to helping others gain sobriety.

In 1986 Jo's dad was afflicted with congestive heart failure. Jo made many, many trips to Huntsville to help her mother take care of him, and I went with her when I was able. Gramper died on October 20th of 1987, just thirteen days after his eightieth birthday. A part of our world was gone.

By 1988 it became apparent that the survival of St. Andrew's was seriously threatened, and the stress showed in its members. Jo and I were very thankful that the members did not blame us for the church's problems. Bishop Stough tried to effect a joining of Trinity and St. Andrew's with St. Mary's of Childersburg, but the people from St. Mary's vetoed the proposition. They had a young priest who worked part-time at the Mental Health Center and part-time at St. Mary's, and they were happy with that arrangement. We decided we had to look for another church, and spent the next two years interviewing. We encountered one of two situations: the churches either could not afford us or they felt I was too old.

Things were happening in the family, also. During the summer of 1988 Mother called from Canada to announce that she had married Donald Foreman. Don had a cottage four doors down from Mother's place. He was five years younger than Mother, recently widowed, and had very poor eyesight due to macular degeneration. Mother felt it was her ministry to take care of him. She said, "You don't seem surprised."

"No, I'm not. He's all you have ever talked about for the past few years."

Mother and Don maintained the twice-yearly journey between

Canada and Alabama, only now they had a stopping place in Sarnia, Ontario at Don's apartment. The marriage put a burden on us of helping with Don's health care, but Don was such a nice guy we didn't mind.

Our family suffered another misfortune in 1989. Gran fell in her kitchen and broke her hip. It's possible that her hip broke before the fall; the orthopedic surgeon said her bone was very porous. She tried, but could not reach the telephone, and she lay on the floor until a service man came the next day and notified neighbors that she wasn't answering the door. The neighbors called police, who broke into the house and had Gran taken to the hospital.

An orthopedic surgeon did a complete hip replacement and Gran began a vigorous program of physical rehabilitation. Jo went to Huntsville to help her mother through the recovery. Gran recovered without any apparent disability. Her doctor told us that, with fractures like hers, small pieces of bone and marrow will enter the bloodstream and reach the brain, causing a stroke or dementia. Fortunately, Gran did not show any signs of major impairment. The effects that she did exhibit were attributed to her blood pressure medication.

In January of 1990 St. Andrew's held it's annual meeting, and I was later criticized for the way I handled the election of Senior Warden. I would not allow the first nominee to be voted in by acclamation, but asked for more nominations from the floor. The person originally nominated was nearly blind and in poor health, and I was doubtful of his ability to handle the position, especially if he needed to conduct services or meetings. A second person was nominated and elected. Late that night a woman member phoned me at home and expressed her anger at "my stabbing (name withheld) in the back." Earlier, the treasurer had told me that they did not think they would be able to pay me after July. I felt the time had come for us to leave. I would soon be sixty-two and eligible for reduced social security and a small pension from the church. The following Sunday I announced my intention to retire at the end of July.

For my retirement on July 31st, the Church gave us a really nice pool party at Bob Green's house, and presented us with an oil painting of St. Andrew's Church. The previous Sunday, Trinity, Alpine had hosted a farewell reception for us and had given us a picture of their church.

24 – Back Into Space

Not happy with the prospects of retirement, I decided to continue looking for another church. The end of July came and I had not applied for retirement, so we lived on our savings and the honoraria I received from supply work (filling an empty pulpit in another church). In the summer of 1991 Jo and I visited a church in Florida we really liked. We had lunch with the Senior Warden, got set up for the interview process, and had subsequent telephone interviews. It looked like we were going to find a home at last. The night before our trip for the final interview, the Senior Warden called, in tears as he told us that their bishop had canceled the interview. I wanted to find out why.

I had heard of people being hurt by bad data obtained during background checks, and I felt I had better find out if there was any false information on file about me anywhere. I talked to our Bishop, Bob Miller, and asked him to find out why my interview was canceled. A week or so later Bishop Miller called me and said the other bishop felt that I was too old to take on that church. I told him, "It sounds like we've got the basis for a good equal employment opportunity lawsuit here."

"Oh no! We don't want to do anything like that!"

"Don't worry. I don't want anything I cannot get on my own merits. But I tell you, sir, there is more justice in the business world than in the Church, and the Church should be the paradigm of justice."

I was angry. We really liked that church and wanted to go there. **God had other plans for us.**

I guess more to prove my point than anything else, I called Ken Rogers, one of my former supervisors at Boeing, who was in Huntsville working on the Space Station, and asked him if they had any openings. "No, we've got a hiring freeze right now, but send me a resumé anyway."

A few weeks later I got a call from Boeing to arrange an interview. It was most interesting that they were not interested in my engineering skills, but in my proficiency with a desktop computer. They offered me a job working on the Space Station's weight and resources reduction program, at the maximum increase they were allowed to offer over my last salary. I rather enjoyed being able to back up what I had said about private sector justice being broader that the Church's.

But, wouldn't you know that something like this would happen? The church in Millbrook, a small town outside Montgomery, came through with a reasonable offer, combining their stipend with my retirement pay. Jo and I prayed and discussed the situation thoroughly, but couldn't reach any kind of conclusion. Finally, I said, "Let's just pray quietly for a while and then we'll each write on a slip of paper where we think we should go." We did, then showed each other the slips of paper. They both said "Huntsville." I set off on my sixty-third birthday to go back to Boeing.

I got to Boeing early in the morning and went through an agonizing reassessment of my decision. When the gates opened, I decided to turn the job down and go back to Sylacauga. I went to the personnel department and told them what I wanted to do. The young lady there said she couldn't take care of what I wanted, that my personnel representative was not in that day, and I would have to handle it through my supervisor. I gulped and allowed myself to be led away to report to Ken. I told Ken that I was sorry, but I did not feel right about taking the job. He figuratively twisted my arm and pleaded with me to give it a thirty-day try. I caved in and agreed.

That afternoon I became quite ill and went "home" to Gran's house. By night, I was getting worse. I called Jo and asked her to make an appointment with our doctor, that I would be coming home early in the morning. It turned out I had a nasty sinus infection that laid me up for over a week. I thought surely that would settle the issue with Boeing, but they held the job open for me until I was well enough to work.

After that experience we decided to do things differently. Instead of me going to Huntsville alone and returning home on weekends, Jo came with me and we both stayed with Gran. While I worked during the day, Jo looked at houses, one of her favourite pastimes. She found a nice three-bedroom house for us on Amberwood Drive, in Harvest. We left our house in Sylacauga, moved to Harvest, and prayed for a quick property sale.

Remember that I said, *"God had other plans for us."* We found it remarkable that circumstances had stacked up causing us to return to Huntsville. One of the blessings in store for us was this: When I left Boeing in 1974, I had a vested interest in their pension plan, which would have given me a small monthly sum. By going back to Boeing in 1991, I came under their revised pension plan rules, which would give me six times the amount of money for two more years of work. ***God was seeing our future needs and meeting them*** despite my pigheadedness.

We received another blessing. After I left St. Andrew's, my brother clergy kept me busy filling empty pulpits, so I had the rewarding experience of serving many different churches as well as holding down a full-time job.

The spring of 1992 brought the beginning of a chain of painful events. We got a call from Gran that her refrigerator had quit working. We had a little refrigerator that Jenifer had used at Sewanee, and took it to Gran so she could keep her food cold. As soon as we got things set up, her refrigerator started running again. Stuck thermostat, overheated circuit breaker or something, we didn't know, but it kept on running. After that, we went with Gran to the backyard to look at her flowers. On the way back to the house, Gran stumbled on the edge of the sidewalk and fell. Her shoulder was hurting, so we took her to the hospital. She had fractured her shoulder. Her orthopedic surgeon reset the bone and she physically recovered from the fall, but started acting strangely after that. Small things at first, like buying the same things over and over again on shopping trips when they weren't needed. Her ability to reason became increasingly questionable. Her behaviour became more erratic, and Jo had her hospitalized. Cat scans revealed blockages in several areas of the brain. Apparently, bone fragments and marrow from the shoulder fracture had entered her bloodstream. We needed to get Gran into a care facility. The nearest available facility was Bryce Hospital in Tuscaloosa, 150 miles from Huntsville. It was most painful for Jo and me to see Gran in her condition. Her recent memories were gone. Gran was living back in the "Forties," she thought she was a German prisoner of war, and the only way she could relate to Jo was to think of her as her sister.

In addition to all of this, we found out that the bone in Jo's lower jaw had shrunk to the point where it would no longer support a denture plate. The only good solution was to have a titanium device implanted in her jaw to support and retain a plate. She decided to go ahead with the procedure, which involved two separate surgeries on her lower jaw. This meant a series of trips to Birmingham to an oral surgeon, plus several trips to her dentist in Sylacauga to be fitted with new dentures. It was a drawn out, painful process, but Jo undertook it without a word of complaint or hesitation.

25 – Re-entry

William Clinton took office as President of the United States in January of 1993. This had a serious effect on the Space Station program. The name was changed from "Freedom" to "International Space Station." A shakeup in the program resulted in a realignment of participation by foreign partners, and the need for redesign. We had already gone through one redesign phase and I did not relish having to go through another based solely on political considerations. The change from a Republican to a Democratic administration and Congress caused a serious upheaval in the whole aerospace industry. One of the results was a forced reduction of employees by government contractors. Boeing met this situation by encouraging the retirement of eligible employees. I was close to sixty-five and, as I said, I did not want to go through the headaches of another redesign phase, so I volunteered to retire immediately after my sixty-fifth birthday. My manager wasn't happy. "The invitation to retire was not meant for you!" I was pleased that he considered me too valuable to let go, but I felt that it was the right time and the right decision. I retired from Boeing in August of 1993. Now I would have more time to be with Jo on the long trips to visit her mother, and have more time for church work.

1994 started off with a bang. Jo was sitting at my desk and found an Amsler Grid under the desk pad.

"What is this for?"

"They use it to test for macular degeneration." After Don married Mother, I learned what I could about the disease to better help and care for him. I still had the grid used for diagnosis.

"How does it work?"

"You focus one eye at a time on the target in the center. If the rest of the grid looks like a series of squares, you are alright. If any of the little squares are distorted or have wavy lines, you have a distortion or degeneration of the macula. Let me show you how."

I looked at the grid with my right eye and saw distorted squares! My pulse rate went up considerably. I immediately scheduled an eye exam.

The examination revealed diabetic retinopathy in the right eye. This explained why I had problems aligning images on a computer graphics screen. The damage to the eye was old, and subsequent medical tests for diabetes were negative. I had high blood pressure and was given medication for that. My ophthalmologist performed laser surgery on the eye to remove the aneurysms that were causing the visual distortion, but there were two he didn't remove, because they were too close to the macula.

I found that being a retired priest provided me a degree of desirability. Many small churches could not afford a full-time priest, but could afford a retired one. I started getting inquiries about my availability, and answered some of the solicitations. Filling empty pulpits kept me busy and provided a small, but helpful income. During the four years after leaving St. Andrew's, I served in fourteen different churches.

When we first went to Huntsville in 1964 we joined St. Christopher's Church, the mission meeting in the house behind ours. In time, St. Christopher's built their new church. By 1972 IBM had greatly diminished their participation in the space program. This, and cutbacks by other contractors, caused such a loss of members that St. Christopher's was no longer self-supporting. The people of St. Christopher's met this challenge by selling their building and merging with the congregation of Holy Cross Chapel at Alabama A&M University, the formerly all black college. This was the birth of Holy Cross-St. Christopher's, a racially mixed congregation that met and worshiped in a lovely A-frame chapel near the campus.

During the summer of 1994 Holy Cross-St. Christopher's was without a priest and did not have sufficient income to employ one full-time. I started serving there, first as a supply priest in August, then as priest-in-charge in November. I could not be rector, because I was officially retired and could not gain tenure. I enjoyed being their priest, especially since I had been a member of St. Christopher's thirty years earlier. I knew a lot of the people, and the church was large enough to support good programs. By only working part-time, I was not a drain on their budget, yet I had a church of my own to serve. I was enjoying an active retirement, and I told Bishop Parsley, the Bishop of Alabama, that I felt like I had the best of both worlds.

We had a time of sadness in July 1994. Doyle Nicely, John Nicely's father, died on July 20th. I had the privilege of giving the eulogy at his burial service on the 23rd.

26 – Florida Re-visited

All of Gran's legal issues were pretty well resolved. It was time to give Jo a much-deserved vacation, especially since she had borne the brunt of her mother's care. I remembered how fond she was of the Atlantic Ocean north of Daytona Beach. Five years before, we had interviewed at St. Mark's Church in Palatka, Florida and they recommended we visit Crescent Beach before going back home. We did, and we liked the area. With this in mind, I picked up the AAA Tour Book and found Crescent Beach. They had a listing for Beacher's Lodge, a condominium/hotel on the ocean. It was the only listing that wasn't a motel. I reserved a studio unit and off we went.

The studio unit was big enough, but it did not face the ocean and only had a bedroom, kitchenette, and bath, so I asked the manager to show us a queen unit, which had a bedroom, living/dining room, kitchen, bath, and a balcony on the ocean side. She showed us one and I said, "We'll take it."

Jo looked like a child at Christmas, and said, "Really, can we have this?" One of the many things that I treasured about Jo was she did not have to have the best of everything, but when she got more than she expected, she was childlike in her appreciation.

We enjoyed our stay at Beacher's so much that we stayed an extra two days and made a week of it. This was the first of many trips to Beacher's, and the start of serious thought about moving to Florida. I later found out, and thought it ***most remarkable***, that this was the only year that Beacher's had advertised in the AAA Tour Book. I wonder what the result would have been had we just gone to a motel.

November 1994 through January 1995 was relatively uneventful. We had a good holiday season and things were going well at Holy Cross-St. Christopher's.

February was a different story. On February 10th Don had a heart attack while outdoors in the bitter cold of Sarnia, Ontario. He lay on the ground at the apartment building's back entrance for some time before a neighbor entering the building found him and called for help. Medics got him to the hospital, but he was in a coma. Don died on the 15th. He was eighty-four years old. We went to Sarnia the next day. I officiated at Don's funeral on the 18th and his burial on the 20th. We stayed in Sarnia until the 21st to help Mother get things squared away. Much to our dismay, we found that Mother was not in very good condition herself. She did not appear strong enough to be living alone. Sister Sharon and her family, Jo and I talked Mother into going into an assisted living facility. She wanted to go to Huntsville with us, but Sharon persuaded her to go to Brighton, so she could be close to four of her six grandchildren. Sharon took Mother to Brighton and moved her into The Village, a retirement and nursing home. We went home and tried to pick up our lives again.

Jenifer and Larry came in April and helped us conduct a big yard sale at Gran's house. By the end of the month we had a contract to sell Gran's house, so we were making good progress in taking care of her affairs.

In May we took our first serious trip house hunting in Florida. We went to Crystal River, Citrus Springs, Dade City, and St. Augustine.

While in Florida, we retrieved a call on our answering machine from Mike Wilson, Jo's former boss at WNDA, calling to see if we were alright. A tornado had hit Harvest on the 18th and done horrendous damage. We got on the phone and found out that our house was not damaged, but that our farm was torn up. Two thirds of our eight-acre pine and hardwood forest was destroyed. Most of the trees were uprooted, and the ground disturbance choked the spring and changed the course of the creek. This was the third time our farm had been hit in twenty-five years. We decided not to build on the farm.

27 – Control Issues

By June serious storm clouds of a different nature were forming. Sharon called, asking me to give her all of Mother's account numbers. She said she wanted to manage the funds in a way that would qualify Mother for Medicaid. Meanwhile, Mother had called me and said, "Sharon is raising all kinds of hell because I gave you power of attorney." I consulted our attorney, who had considerable experience in handling family matters. He advised me to be very cautious, and to have their requests sent to him.

On the 14th I went to Brighton to meet with Sharon, her older daughter, Renée, and their attorney. The attorney asked Mother if having me as attorney-in-fact was what she wanted. She said, "Yes." I left there with the impression that Sharon's attorney was going to present us with a plan for administering Mother's finances that would give us the greatest benefit.

Shortly after my return home, Mother called, asking me how to contact the police, because of the way Sharon was treating her. Jo and I talked things over, consulted our attorney, who I had also retained for Mother, and decided it would be better for her to come and stay with us. Mother was enthusiastic about the prospect. She did not want me to say anything to Sharon, and I abided by her wish. Our attorney concurred and told us not to say anything until we were ready to leave Brighton.

On the 6th of July I was getting ready to leave for Brighton, when a registered letter came from Sharon's attorney. I thought it might be a financial proposal. Instead it was a notification that they were going to have Mother cancel my power of attorney and give complete control of everything to Sharon. I asked our attorney to give them a reply and I left for Brighton.

I brought Mother home with me on the 7th. I asked her if she would tell Sharon that she was leaving, and she adamantly said, "No." On the trip to Huntsville I noted that Mother had memory problems. Some of her recollections of family involvement in World War II were rather bizarre.

Understandably, Sharon came unglued when she discovered that Mother was gone. I patiently endured an hour and a half of vitriol at three o'clock the next morning, hoping that by letting her vent her anger we could eventually talk. I told her, "I hope that you can forgive me, put this behind us, and get on with our lives."

Her reply was, "I can never forgive you."

"Well, I'm sure that God forgives me."

"No, God will never forgive you. You have committed an unforgivable sin."

I felt awful, not for my sake, but for hers, because I knew too well the damage that comes from a lack of forgiveness.

Mother was doing pretty well with us. We put her in the care of a doctor well versed in geriatric medicine. She received in-home nursing care and physical therapy. We made no attempt to limit her contact with Sharon and Sharon's family, despite the many haranguing and pleading phone calls from them. One disturbing call caused Mother to become faint and we called the EMT's. She recovered sufficiently to not require hospitalization.

Mother decided she needed to set us free and go into an assisted care facility. We set her up with Wyndham Park, a highly rated place near our home. On the 24th of August, the day before she was to move, she got a card from Sharon and Sharon's children telling her how much they missed her. She stayed up nearly all night reading and rereading that card. The next morning she became faint, and we called the EMT's again. The first thing the EMT said was, "Have you been talking to your daughter again?"

Mother did not recover this time, and was taken to the hospital. The neurosurgeon found that Mother had a constricted artery at the base of her skull, and stress aggravated it. They prescribed blood thinners, but her doctor would not release her to go to Wyndham Park, because they did not have a full-time RN. She would have to go into a nursing home. I checked out the available nursing home and it made me ill. She could not have her own doctor and would have to use the nursing home's doctor. The toilets were raised quite high and there were no tubs, only showers. I believed Mother would never understand why she had to be there.

Sharon talked to Mother at length the night before she was to be released. The report I got from Mother was, "I think Sharon has changed. Perhaps I should go back with her." I was elated. I wanted nothing more see than to see us all reconciled. I talked it over with Sharon, and she arranged for Mother to return to The Village in Brighton.

Mother was discharged from the hospital on September 1st to go home with me. We got her stabilized at home and left for Brighton five days later. We stopped overnight on the way to Brighton. The next morning when we stopped for breakfast, Mother said, "I really do not feel good about going back."

"Mother, you cannot do this. All the arrangements have been made, and we really have no alternative."

When we got to The Village, Mother walked right away from us and went to the Catholic service that was being held. She was not one bit happy about being back with Sharon or being back at The Village. Sharon was talkative, polite, but somewhat cool. We had lunch together, and just before I left for home she gave me a kiss on the cheek that left me with a cold feeling.

During September, October and November I had frequent conversations with Sharon, and I hoped to hear from her about some plan for Mother's care. Sharon's husband, John, had serious health problems. Colon cancer was suspected.

In December I discovered that Sharon had surreptitiously diverted Mother's dividend check from Kellogg Company to her own bank account. At the same time, John was supposed to go into the hospital for a diagnostic procedure. I asked Sharon to let me know the results. She did not call me, and she never talked with me again until I called her late in 2006 to tell her that Jo had passed away. I found out from Mother that John did have cancer and that it was pretty far advanced.

1996 – The New Year began with more than one bang. On January 12th I received registered mail from John Brower, an attorney in Brighton, Michigan, notifying me that Mother had set up a trust fund and that I was to turn over all of her assets, and give a complete accounting, not only of her transactions, but our property transactions and Jenifer and Larry's property transactions. The accompanying letter was abusive and suggested suspicion that I had misappropriated funds. All this was to be done in fifteen days, and I was not to be given any knowledge of the contents or provisions of the trust. There was a "terror clause" in the trust stipulating that if I questioned the trust in any way, I would lose any benefit provided for me. I immediately contacted the attorney that I had engaged for my mother and laid the issue before him. He referred me to an attorney in Southfield, Michigan to act on my behalf. We set up a challenge based upon Mother being mentally incompetent; a geriatric doctor had diagnosed her earlier as having

Alzheimer's disease symptoms.

The following Sunday I told the congregation at Holy Cross-St. Christopher's about the situation. "I am all too well aware that scripture says, 'When one of you has a grievance against a brother, does he dare go to law before the unrighteous instead of the saints,' (*I Corinthians 6:1, RSV*) but I feel that I have no other choice except to seek a remedy through law. I feel this situation could greatly hamper my ability to serve you, and, if you think it best, I will resign my position as your pastor." After the service, fully half of the people there said they had been involved in similar bitter family situations. They did not want me to leave, and they promised their support in whatever way possible. This greatly enheartened me.

Our first court appearance was on February 27th, in Howell, Michigan. Mother had recently fallen and broken her hip. She was in the hospital recovering from surgery to repair the fracture. This put the legal situation in a different light; Mother would not, could not be available for any testimony. Initial judgment by the Probate Court was that Mother needed a guardian, that I would retain power of attorney, and that my attorney should seek a court order to open the trust. The Friend of the Court recommended that either Sharon or her daughter, Renée, should be guardian. We agreed to let Sharon be Mother's guardian.

Along with all that we were dealing with in Michigan, Gran's dementia was progressing and had reached a point where she could no longer swallow. They inserted a feeding tube into her stomach and she was transferred to the Alice Kidd nursing care facility at Bryce. Gran died on April 1st, just thirty-six days shy of her eighty-first birthday. I had to be in Michigan for a court hearing on April 2nd, so Jo had to handle Gran's arrangements by herself. Fortunately most of the arrangements had been preplanned.

At the hearing, Sharon, acting as guardian, obtained the trust papers from the attorneys, who had drawn up the trust and were co-trustees, and turned the papers over to the court. A proposal was made that I be named a co-trustee along with Renée. We examined the documents, decided we could live with the trust as it was written, and agreed to let the two attorneys continue as trustees-pro-tem until the trust was accepted by the Probate Court.

28 – Bane and Blessing

On the 4th of April, 1996 we tearfully laid Gran to rest next to Gramper at Madison Crossroads Cemetery. Easter Sunday was on the 7th, and we gratefully celebrated the day with church and then dinner with John and Mary Nicely. Our breather was destined to be brief, though. A routine eye exam on the 23rd revealed that I had glaucoma. I had read about this condition in childhood and it was something I was really afraid of. Going blind was my worst childhood fear. I wondered how many more of my worst fears I would encounter. We went to Beacher's for a five-day stay to get our minds off this latest problem. The ocean is terrific medicine.

Upon our return we settled down to taking care of Gran's estate and trying to get Mother's trust approved by the court in Michigan. We got along without undue complications until September. Sharon's husband, John, died on the 6th. Mother's condition was deteriorating rapidly. She was no longer able to swallow and had a tube inserted for feeding. The last time I talked with her on the telephone she was barely coherent. I made plans to go to Brighton immediately to see her.

We went to Jenifer and Larry's in Huntington, West Virginia on the 29th. Jo would stay there while I went to Brighton. On the 30th Renée called. Mother had died. I immediately went back home to get proper clothing for the funeral, and left Huntsville for Brighton on the 3rd of October.

Mother's burial service was held at the Methodist Church in Brighton. Both trustees met with me at the funeral home and apologized for the problems they had given me. They told my lawyer, "His sister flamboozled us!" Then things turned ugly. A provision in the trust allowed tuition gifts for grandchildren for higher education. The trustees denied Sharon's application for grants because of the high legal expenses caused by her intransigence and the fact that they were only temporary trustees. Sharon countered this by coming up with thirty thousand dollars worth of claims against the estate in favor of her and her younger daughter, Laura.

Sharon persisted in her claims and non-cooperation, causing us great distress, and we focused a lot of anger on her. Then one evening – I'll remember it clearly as long as I have memory – I had ***a flash of revelation*** while Jo and I were in the kitchen talking. "We are not fighting Sharon," I said, "we are fighting Principalities and Powers that are trying to destroy us." (*Ref. Ephesians 8:12, RSV*) We rebuked those malignant forces and immediately felt peace. Our perspective of the whole situation changed and we were able to be more objective and make decisions accordingly. Our freedom from oppression was miraculous.

We made another trip to Florida in early March to get away, renew ourselves and look for a house. We spent three days in Dade City, had a terrific meal at my cousin's restaurant, Kokopeli, and enjoyed a performance of the oratorio "Seven Last Words (of Christ)" at St. Mary's Church. We spent the next week at Beacher's Lodge and looked at a lot of houses and property.

April and May were fairly quiet. We had decided we wanted to leave Huntsville, so we started getting our house ready for sale. By June most of our legal complications were settled and we received a portion of Mother's estate. Now we were in a better position to buy a house.

We thought seriously about moving to Huntington, to be close to Jenifer and Larry. We looked and looked, but houses there were either too expensive or in poor condition. We went back home without making any decision. Though we did not have a specific house purchase in mind, we put our house up for sale on August 23rd.

More sadness – John Nicely's mother, Sally, died on September 9th. I assisted with her burial service on the 12th.

After nearly six months on the market, our house still had not sold, and we thought about "just staying there." Thanksgiving rolled around and we went to Jenifer and Larry's for the holiday. Lo and behold, we got a call from Tommy Pruett, our real estate agent. A family who wanted the house got approval for a mortgage and were ready to buy, but they had to have occupancy in thirty days. We went back to the only house in Huntington that we were even interested in, and decided to make an offer. The offer was acceptable, but the owners were out of town and wouldn't be back for several weeks. There was no way we could get that house in time to move, and the owners were not one bit accommodating. We called Tommy. "You've got to find us a place to live." He came up with numerous listings (a buyer's market can be nice) and we started going to open houses. We settled on a four-bedroom home on Stone Valley Drive, in the village of Monrovia. We were able to make a satisfactory deal and got immediate occupancy. We moved into our "new" home on December 22nd.

1997 closed on a sad note: Bill Taylor, my aunt Winnifred's husband, died on New Year's Eve. I started 1998 by celebrating the Requiem Mass and giving the eulogy for Uncle Bill at St. Mary's in Dade City.

We took our farm off the market, since there had been little activity, the listing term had expired, and the only interested prospect could not get the financing he needed. Evidently The Lord had other plans for us. Tommy called and wondered if there was a way we could still make the property available to the prospect. We agreed to rent the property with an option to buy. The prospect accepted the offer, and eventually was able to get the financing he needed to buy the property. This was the second time within a year that we got an offer to buy on real estate just after we decided we would leave things as they were.

We started modifying our new home for comfort and appearance. By June we had purchased some new furniture, paved the areas under the back porch and deck, and turned the back porch into a sun room.

September brought another change into our life. Jean Lowe died on September 2nd. We had known Jean and her daughter, Linda, for twenty-five years. Jean had a powerful healing ministry in Huntsville, and Linda had worked with Jo at WNDA. Jo had given Linda considerable help in opening a Christian bookstore, and Jenifer had her first paying job there. As a consequence, Jo and the Lowe's became very close friends. Linda was epileptic and had quite limited capabilities, but believed she could "do all things in Him who strengthens [me]." (*Philippians 4:13, RSV*)

At Jean's burial in Maple Hill Cemetery, Joyce Daniels, the senior warden of St. Stephen's Church, asked me to consider becoming their interim rector. I talked with their vestry and they offered me the position. This was a welcome opportunity for me. St. Stephen's was a large church with an excellent music program, an active lay ministry, and a day school. I knew it would soon be time for me to retire completely, and this would be a way for me to close out with a large church and a dynamic group of people that we had known for many years. I accepted the offer and arranged to leave Holy Cross-St. Christopher's at the end of November.

Living in Florida was still very much in our plans. We went to St. Augustine in October and paid for an option to buy a lot in Cypress Point Phase II. This was really looking ahead; the roads in the subdivision were not paved, and the county had not approved the subdivision plan.

The rest of 1998 was pretty normal. There were weddings, baptisms, confirmations and funerals, and the constant tasks of house and yard maintenance.

1998 did end spectacularly. An ice storm started the morning of December 23rd. I had a miserable cold and it didn't take much persuasion to get me to stay home and not go to the office. The storm continued all day and into the night. At four o'clock in the morning on the 24th we awoke to the sounds of tree branches hitting the roof. I got up, dressed, and went outside to see if the cars were in the open. It sounded like a war zone outside! Tree branches were breaking off everywhere. There were limbs all over the garage roof, one of them had punched through the roof and ceiling, and limbs were bouncing off the roof and hitting the cars. The ice was very thick and reminded me of the storm we had in Sylacauga. The power went off at four-forty-five in the morning. Conditions were so bad that we canceled the Midnight Mass at St. Stephen's. I felt terrible about not having a Christmas Mass for the first time in seventeen years as a priest.

Christmas was cold and dark. Dinner was hot dogs and beans. Fortunately, we had logs for the fireplace and bottled gas for our lantern and camp stove. The day after Christmas we spent replenishing our bottled gas and firewood, and getting KFC chicken dinners. Hats off to Huntsville Utilities! They had our power back on by four o'clock that afternoon.

29 – Leaving Huntsville

1999 was another year with sad beginnings. Fr. George Wood died on January 5th. Fr. Wood had been a chaplain for the 82nd Airborne Division during World War II. He was a rather famous person; he had jumped with members of the 82nd at Bastogne, and was portrayed in the movie <u>Battle of the Bulge</u>. Fr. Wood was an Associate Priest at Nativity, and we had known him since before we went to seminary. He was much loved. Gramper, who was very proud of his own service in Europe during World War II, really liked Fr. George and loved to hear him preach.

Jim Wallace, a former friend and engineer at Boeing, died on the 8th.

Mary Nicely's brother, Leonard Melton, died on the 17th.

St. Stephen's finished their search for a new rector. Fr. Jake Owensby was due to start on March 1st, and I was to work out the rest of my contract as an assistant. February 28th was my last service there as their rector. They had a lovely reception for Jo and me after the service. It was ***truly a blessing*** to spend one of my last active years as a priest at St. Stephen's.

Our roof damage from the Christmas Eve storm was repaired in April. The contractor could not get matching shingles, so they replaced the whole roof. We paid one-third of the cost; the insurance company paid the rest. I installed new roof fans and did a lot of cosmetic repair inside.

Jenifer and Larry came to visit on May 12th. Larry had to leave on the 16th, but Jen stayed on until the end of the month and we held a rather impressive yard sale. It seemed like all of our efforts this year had been to get our house in first class condition and pare down our belongings.

We visited St. Augustine in August, which was beginning to be part of our routine. Back home I continued doing supply work and assisting at St. Stephen's.

On October 19th Richard Brian called. His mother, Mona Molnar, had died from cancer. I went to Chelsea, Michigan to attend Mona's funeral on the 23rd and be with Richard.

In December we found out that Jamie, our 16-pound, part Maine Coon tabby, had cholangial hepatitis, and we began a regimen of prednisone therapy. We had adopted Jamie as a kitten, and he was now almost ten years old. He had been a really fun cat to own, except we didn't own him near as much as he owned us. He sang like no other cat we ever had and could jump five feet into the air.

We closed out 1999 with a Christmas visit to Jenifer and Larry's.

Richard called on the 10th of January, 2000 to tell us that Steve Molner, Mona's husband, had died. It was a blessed relief in many ways; he was severely incapacitated and wheelchair bound.

In mid-April we went to our favourite spot – Beacher's Lodge. We looked at the lot we had selected and at houses built by Lee Kidd. On the 17th we signed a contract to buy Lot #34, then spent time with Lee Kidd to discuss building our house. We didn't like any of the plans he was using, so we decided to design the house ourselves. We spent the rest of the month in Dade City with Uncle Harold and Aunt Babs, and Aunt Winnifred. In June we visited Jenifer and Larry.

July brought more sad news. Ken Rogers, a longtime friend and former boss at Boeing, suffered a series of strokes and was hospitalized. Ken died on the 21st. We had lost a dear friend.

At the end of the month, Lee Kidd sent us a building proposal using our house plan. The proposal was acceptable to us, so we signed a contract with Lee. We were off and running.

August was especially hot, and we noted that Jamie was sleeping a lot and staying under the car in the garage. We thought he was just trying to beat the heat, but then he did not show up one morning. We began a frantic search, including making many trips to the animal shelters, putting up posters in veterinary clinics, placing ads in the paper, all to no avail. Our hearts were broken once again. Our vet speculated that the prednisone treatments had taken a toll on his kidneys, and that Jamie just went off into the woods to die alone.

August through November we spent getting our vehicles ready for the move to Florida, sprucing up the house and yard, buying furniture for the new house, hosting a monster yard sale, taking care of dental work, and getting new glasses. In addition, I continued doing supply work in Huntsville and Tennessee.

December was busy, busy, busy. We went to St. Augustine to see the progress on the house and to select fixtures, cabinets, floor coverings, etc.

Jenifer and Larry came on the 20th to spend Christmas with us back in Huntsville. We went to St. Mary Magdalene's Church in

Fayetteville, where I celebrated Midnight Mass on Christmas Eve. I was very tired, my left knee was bothering me, and I felt like I had not given the people what used to be my best. I talked with Jo later and told her, "I think my preaching days are coming to an end. I just can't give what I think I should." She said she had noticed that I was not doing well, and agreed that maybe it was time to take it easy.

We greeted the Third Millennium with two inches of pretty, white snow. A few days later our new computer arrived from Dell, and the cartons we had ordered for packing. Most of our energy and thought now focused on the move to Florida. We spent our days, and some of the nights, buying light fixtures for the new house, making more furniture decisions, and still taking care of parishioners' needs. We went to St. Augustine during the last week of February to finalize our floor covering selections and deliver the fixtures we had bought. With building nearing completion, we put our Stone Valley house on the market with Tommy.

We did a lot of praying about our housing situation. The new house would be completed in two months, and we didn't want to leave our house in Huntsville vacant. During March and early April we had eight showings with different agents. On the 8th of April, Tommy brought us an offer. We believed ***our prayers had truly been answered.*** We sold the house within six weeks, the buyers were devout Christians, which pleased us, and there was no bargaining over price.

On May 4th I took a lot of clothing to Jenifer's to sell in a consignment shop in Huntington. Jenifer came home with me on the 5th to help us pack and move.

May 9th brought conflicting emotions. We were excited about our new house in Florida, but remorseful about leaving Alabama, our home state for thirty-seven years. Ashley, our old collie, was drinking a lot of water, not eating, and barely able to stand. One morning she did not recognize Jenifer and tried to attack her. The day before we were to leave, we took her to the vet to see if she could make the trip. She had to be lifted into the van and cried all the way to the clinic. When we got there, she put her head down and pushed tightly into a corner. The vet said it looked like she was trying to tell us something. The vet checked her over and said she thought Ashley was shutting down. It was like she was telling us she was ready to go. We decided that the best thing we could do for her was put her to rest. It reminded us of what Ed Mac Moore, our vet in Sylacauga, had said. He took care of Meg, our

Keeshond, and three cats for us, including Frances. Frances needed a lot of medical care, and we asked Ed Mac about the prognosis. He said, "When she is ready to go, she will let you know." And she did. She was eighteen years old. We had a similar experience with Meg, and now with Ashley.

We left Huntsville on the 10th of May, with Jo and Jen in the Voyager and me in the Fifth Avenue.

30 – Beginnings in Florida

We reached St. Augustine on May 11th and stayed at Beacher's Lodge until the movers arrived. It was Jenifer's first stay at Beacher's and she really loved it. We enjoyed the beach and restaurants in St. Augustine for the next three days, and then the van arrived and our work began anew. After the first couple of days in the new house, we balanced our work with trips to Crescent Beach, Matanzas Inlet, and Fort Matanzas. Jenifer indulged her love of body surfing every chance she got. Jenifer left for home on the 20th, and Jo and I settled in doing all the things it takes to make a house a home.

And then, the fun started. Our water was tainted with black sediment. We thought at first it was dirt that had gotten into the pipes during the building. It wasn't. Sulfur gas in the water was reacting with the copper pipes to form copper sulfide. We looked at all the options for getting rid of the gas, most of them quite expensive, and finally decided to take our well driller's recommendation to use a shallower well. The water would contain iron, but that could be removed by a water softener. So, we had a new well drilled, and wound up being in that class of people who have separate water systems for their house and their yard.

We spent late spring, the summer, and early fall putting up blinds and shelves, unpacking, planting citrus and ornamental trees, and exploring St. Augustine and the surrounding area. On July 1st we blessed the house and grounds.

One day at Ace Hardware I saw a group gathered around a little TV at the checkout counter. They were talking about a plane hitting a building in New York City. I thought, "Small plane, pilot error." When I got home and turned on the TV, I saw the enormity of the situation. Terrorists had flown two airliners into the twin towers of the World Trade Center. Now we had 9/11/2001 to add to 12/07/41 as a day of infamy. I decided then to stop shopping for a church and go to Reconciliation, the nearest Episcopal church. We had gone to Reconciliation whenever we visited St. Augustine. Jo and I had sponsored the rector, Paul Canepa, and his wife, Jackie, at Seminary of the Southwest in Austin. Much to our dismay, Paul retired just when we moved to St. Augustine, so we had lost interest in Reconciliation and started looking for another church. We tried the church at Federal Point, where Paul was serving, but it was a long drive.

September 14th brought our first real taste of tropical weather. Tropical Storm Gabrielle hit with almost hurricane force winds and buckets of rain. Our pool overflowed, our house and yard were now an island, and we lost power until the next day. Fortunately, our little generator was working and we were able to keep the freezer and refrigerator going. Coleman lamps and a camp stove served us well. Fortunately, the ice storms and tornadoes of Alabama, and our earlier camping days, had taught us how to survive comfortably.

We spent Thanksgiving with Jenifer and Larry in Huntington, West Virginia.

2002 was four days old when we got a taste of North Florida winter. A hard freeze was predicted and it was very windy. We struggled all evening to cover plants, only to have the wind blow all the coverings off during the night.

The next day we went to the CFA Cat Show in Jacksonville, where we succumbed to the wiles of a four-month old female Maine Coon cat we named Lacey (Morekats Touch of Lace). Jo bought Lacey for me as a gift. We both missed Jamie and she knew how fond I am of Maine Coon cats. This was the beginning of a new experience in cat ownership. On our arrival home, Lacey got away from us and crawled under the china cabinet. We unloaded the cabinet and raised it to get her out. She was a trembling, frightened, little wisp of a kitty.

The next day Lacey was still shaking, not eating or drinking, and was running a fever. We took her to a vet, who gave her fluids sub-cutaneously and tube fed her. Our treatment of Lacey afterward, I fear, made a little sick cat into a very spoiled cat. For some reason, the house had become like outdoors for Lacey, and the only time we could hold her was when she was in the bathroom, which had been her room during her first week with us.

The rest of winter and early spring were spent doing what I guess old, retired folks do after they move to Florida. We bought plants and trees, shopped at the outlets and malls, walked the beach, and tried many different restaurants. We had a very nice visit in January from Jim Taylor, the president of Cumberland College in Williamsburg, Kentucky, and his wife, Dinah. Our first contact with the Taylor's was in 1998. We had read about the work that Cumberland and their students do to better the living conditions of the poor in Appalachia, and decided to support the college and its work. In March, Roy Dobyns, President Taylor's assistant, visited.

We enjoyed Lacey's antics, running around in her jungle, our house. She did have digestive problems, which the vet attributed to an infection and treated with antibiotics. The problem would clear up, but recur a month or so later. After a ***lot of prayers*** and a period of observation, we determined that her heartworm preventative was sickening her. We discontinued that medication and her condition cleared up. This meant she would have to be an indoor cat, protected from mosquitoes. This was fine with us. She had the screened pool area for her "outdoors", and we had lost too many outdoor cats in the past.

I started cabinetry projects in April, by building in bookcases in the family room on both sides of the window, and a plant shelf over the window. I enjoy working with wood. I often reflect that Jesus was a carpenter, and working with wood makes me feel close to Him. After I finished the bookcases, I started on cabinets in the garage. I built wall cabinets with sliding doors along two walls, and a broom cabinet near the kitchen door.

Jenifer and Larry came in the middle of June. On the 20th, Jenifer's forty-first birthday, we all had dinner at South Beach Grill, the seaside restaurant beside Beacher's Lodge that we had come to love. That same day, Uncle Harold Cook died of congestive heart failure and emphysema. We were glad that we had all visited him just a few days earlier. I went to Dade City on the 24th to do Harold's burial service.

In July, Jo and I quietly celebrated the forty-five years we had been married and my seventy-fourth birthday.

In August our world started to unravel. An eye examination revealed that my glaucoma was getting worse and required additional medication. Also, a cataract in my right eye was becoming troublesome.

We finished 2002 with a trip to Jenifer and Larry's for Thanksgiving. We got a new water treatment system in December, and Richard Brian came to visit. He was seriously considering moving to Florida, and traveled from our place to Tampa to see what things were like there.

31 – Settling In

We started 2003 off with what seemed like our "settled-in" Florida routine. We continued the struggle to keep plumbing fixtures clean from the heavily calcified water, and I continued my cabinetry. I began doing services at Church in the Pines, a small startup church in Flagler Estates, and supplied for Fr. Burt Froehlich at Reconciliation.

February 1st was a day of shock and tragedy. The space shuttle Columbia (STS107) broke up over Texas at an altitude of 215,000 feet. All seven crewmembers were killed. Even though I was long removed from the space program, it was still very much a part of me.

Visits from Charles and Joan Grover, and friends from Alabama, and a trip to Jenifer and Larry's in Huntington enlivened our days. On July 16th we went to Dade City to celebrate Aunt Winnifred's ninetieth birthday. The rest of the summer was pretty quiet and routine until the 3rd of September, when Aunt Babs, Harold's wife, was found dead in her apartment from a heart attack. It was just a little more than a year since Harold died. I did her burial service in Dade City on the 8th.

Jenifer came for a ten-day visit on October 1st. We spent our time shopping, eating out, and going to the beach. I continued on with my work at Church in the Pines, although attendance had dropped considerably because of the revisionism taking place in the Episcopal Church.

It seemed like each New Year started off with more of a bang than just the fireworks. Jo and I ushered in 2004 with miserable flu symptoms. After we recovered we celebrated by giving our Chrysler Fifth Avenue to the Sheriff's Boys Ranch and buying a new Nissan pickup.

February brought sadness and further realization of the fragility of life. The Rt. Rev. Furman C. Stough died on the 2nd. Bishop Stough had seen us through the whole seminary and ordination process, and occupied a special place in our hearts. On the 4th we got word that The Rev. William Spong had died. Will was a brilliant Pastoral Theology professor. I learned a lot from him in seminary and he had become a special person to me.

Late in February, Charles and Joan Grover visited again. This time they stayed at Beacher's. They had a great time there, and we had a great time with them.

I began a prolonged course of treatment in April to preserve the vision in my right eye. Dr. Paul Hund, of the Eye Center, performed laser surgery around the iris to try to relieve the fluid pressure. The operation was only partially successful. Meanwhile, the vision in that eye was getting worse. Dr. Hund proposed removing the cataract, which he believed would help relieve the fluid pressure and enable him to bring the vision in that eye to 20/40. We went ahead with the cataract removal and lens implant. I was excited about the prospect of good vision in that eye. I knew many people who had cataracts removed and lenses implanted with very good results, and I looked forward to the procedure. The results were quite disappointing. My vision did not improve, but the new lens did provide a clearer window into the eye, and Dr. Hund was able to see an edema mass near the macula, and numerous micro aneurysms. Dr. Hund referred me to Dr. Sullivan at the Florida Retina Institute. Dr. Sullivan was quite optimistic about being able to correct my condition, and administered a series of Kenalog steroid injections in the eye socket. Hopefully this would cause absorption of the edema. Thirty days later, the swelling was down somewhat, but not to the extent that Dr. Sullivan had hoped. However, the vision had improved from 20/200 to 20/80. In the middle of July, Dr. Sullivan performed a laser procedure to try to further stimulate fluid absorption.

Jenifer and Larry came for a week's visit on August 7th. We paid for their stay at Beacher's for the first three days so that they could spend time right on the beach. They stayed with us for the next three days, and we spent the time shopping, eating out, and going to the beach at Matanzas Inlet.

At midnight on the 13th, the last day of their visit, we had our first real taste of a hurricane with Charley, which hit with lots of rain and lightning. Fortunately we suffered no damage, but it was scary. Jenifer went into the front bedroom and saw the windows bowing in from the wind. Larry and I saw the dining room windows bow in.

On September 5th hurricane Frances hit with a fury. We lost power at two in the afternoon, and several tree limbs fell and damaged the pool screen. I had carefully followed the instructions for storing the generator, and wouldn't you know – it wouldn't start. Draining all of the gasoline out had caused an o-ring in the carburetor to dry out. We bought ice to save some of our food. Since the pump for the well is electric, we had no running water, so we hauled water from the pool for washing and toilet flushing. On the 7th we got hit with the trailing edge winds, which were much worse than the leading edge winds. Porch panels tore loose from their tracks. Our lovely pine tree on the eastern edge of the front yard was blown down and missed the house by only three feet. On the 10th we were warned that Ivan was coming and the Keys were being evacuated. We decided to go to a motel while rooms were still available, to escape the heat and humidity and have running water. We were able to get into the Holiday Inn on Anastasia Island. We went to the house to pick up some things, and the power came on. We worked until one o'clock the next morning cleaning out the freezer and the refrigerators, and cooking what meat we thought we could save. Then Jo went back to the motel for the night and I stayed at the house.

We had two weeks of recovery time and then Jeanne hit. Fortunately, we had managed to get the generator running, so we were able to keep essential household services going. On the 26th Jeanne dropped a big tree limb on the pool screen structure, collapsing one of the beams and several purlins.

After all of the hurricane excitement subsided we went back to taking care of business. I visited Dr. Sullivan in late October and my eye had not improved significantly. The edema still remained. He presented me with the remaining option for clearing away the edema, a Kenalog injection into the eye itself. It carried no guarantee of success, and there was the possibility of losing sight in the eye permanently. I declined the treatment.

That night, alone at the dinette table, I heard an inner voice, as if the Lord was talking to me. ***"Are you going to give up and live with your eye the way it is, or will you take the step that may give you healing?"*** It was as if I was being asked whether I trusted or not. The next day I called Dr. Sullivan's office and made an appointment for the Kenalog injection. I underwent the procedure on November 5th. Six weeks later Dr. Sullivan did extensive laser work near the macula to seal off the micro-aneurysms.

By mid January of 2005 my right eye started showing some improvement. The swelling was going down and vision was 20/80. By the end of February I was able to go to church again, but I experienced a setback in March. My vision improved to 20/60, but the pressure had increased to a dangerous level. This is one of the hazards of intra-ocular steroid therapy. The doctor put me on Diamox to reduce the pressure, but I suffered bad side affects from it. At one point I asked the doctor what my vision was, and he replied, "We are not even concerned about what your vision is. We are concerned about saving it." By the end of April the pressure was down to an acceptable level and my vision was holding at 20/60.

In mid-May we took Lacey to the vet to check an intestinal problem. The vet prescribed an antibiotic in pill form, and this is the point where I experienced some ***divine intervention***. The vet asked, "Would you like me to show you how to give her the pills?"

We pilled so many cats and dogs it's a wonder I didn't say, "We know how to do that." Instead, I said, "Yes." When the vet opened the cat's mouth wide, she noticed a large growth, the size of a small grape, on Lacey's tongue, down deep in her throat. We had it removed and had a biopsy done. It was an eosinophilic granuloma, a lesion associated with allergic reactions, and was, fortunately, benign. I dread to think of the consequences had I been my usual know-it-all self.

July brought the good news that the edema was gone from my right eye and the pressure was normal. July also brought a two-week visit from Jenifer. We did have fun shopping, beaching, and eating. Jenifer added to her salt-water "experience" by being stung by a jellyfish.

August was uneventful until the 25th, when hurricane Katrina crossed Florida and entered the Gulf of Mexico. Katrina hit the Gulf Coast and New Orleans on the 28th and 29th. The levees failed on the 30th and New Orleans was flooded. Although we were not hit directly by Katrina, we felt sorry for the people who were, because of the pain we knew they were suffering.

For Thanksgiving we went to Huntington to celebrate with Jenifer and Larry. By this time my right eye was much better. The pressure was down and the vision was about 20/40, as good as we could expect.

In early December, Jo fell beside her bed and strained her back. We took no special note whether she had blacked out or just tripped, as the back pain overshadowed everything else. As I look back, I wonder if that wasn't a precursor of what was coming during the next year.

We started 2006 in a very ambitious frame of mind. We planned to rearrange our shared office to give Jo a better sewing and craft center. We ordered a lovely cherry desk, hutch, and return from Staples to replace her old computer desk and sewing table. The furniture had to be assembled, but that was fine. It was the kind of task I enjoyed.

In February we got the very good news from Dr. Sullivan that everything looked good, except he was concerned that a carotid condition could have caused my problems. He referred me for an ultrasound. Other than that, he did not want to see me again for another year. We felt like we were getting a new lease on life.

By March, Jo had moved into her new work center. She really loved it. I was glad she did, and glad that we had done it. It was almost like we were running in high gear once we finished with the eye therapies. We gave little thought to the carotid concern.

The swimming pool became our next project. We put up small floodlights to light the yard around the pool enclosure, and had a solar pool heater installed. I bought a new pressure washer and we started a complete cleaning job on the pool and enclosure. We wanted to have everything just right when Jenifer and Larry came later in the summer. Our life continued on. We shopped, did maintenance, enjoyed the pool, and had our annual visit from Jim and Dinah Taylor.

Jo's shopping ventures hit a peak on July 13th. Royal Doulton, her favourite china company, was closing their outlet store and everything was on sale. We walked out with two big bags full of china. As we approached the car, Jo was talking about a teapot she really liked, but knew she didn't need. I said, "Let's go back and get it." We did. The clerk said she was so glad that Jo had come back for it, that it seemed meant for her. I am so thankful today that I insisted she get that teapot. It made her very happy. She was so full of life and anticipation. Little did we know there would be no more of those little happy times.

32 – Our World is Shattered

As long as I have life and memory I will remember July 19, 2006. I was having coffee and reading the paper at eight in the morning when Jo walked down the hall to the bathroom. She said, "I've been on the computer from three o'clock until five. If you don't mind, I'll go back to bed and try to get some sleep."

"Go ahead, I don't mind."

For some reason or other, I did not get up and get busy right after finishing the paper as I usually did. I heard Jo fall at ten o'clock. I ran to her room and found her on her knees. "My right leg gave out!" she said. I got her up and helped her out to the dinette table. By then she had pretty well recovered the use of her leg. We ran through the three things that are supposed to tell you if a person has had a stroke. Smile, speak a whole sentence, and raise both arms up straight. She handled them without any problem. She said she felt tired and wanted to go back to bed. She got up around two-thirty in the afternoon, was walking alright, but was having trouble putting words together. After having a cup of coffee, she got up and started sorting through the utensils in the draining rack on the sink.

"What are you doing, taking inventory?"

"Yes."

After a little while she came back and sat down at the table. About five o'clock her speech was becoming slurred and broken. It was apparent that things were not going well.

"Maybe we better get you to the hospital."

"No!" (Most emphatically) "No!"

I called Jenifer, and Jo talked with both Jenifer and Larry. They were adamant about the need to get her to the hospital. She was just as adamant in her refusal to go. I started having chest pains and was getting quite anxious. "Please, if you won't go for your sake, please go for mine." She agreed and I called 911. When the EMT's arrived, her blood pressure was 254/150 and her blood sugar was 154. They immediately started treating her blood pressure and took her to the emergency room at Flagler Hospital.

Jo spent the night in ER and had two cat scans, which showed no cerebral bleeding. They started getting her blood pressure down, but she showed increased weakness on her right side and in her speaking. They put her in ICU at midnight. July 20, 2006 marked forty-nine years for Jo and me. What a way to spend an anniversary. They did MRI's, ultrasounds, and a chest X-Ray. Overnight her condition deteriorated to the extent that she could not talk, could not swallow, and had lost use of her right arm and leg. Further tests showed a clot in the left anterior portion of her brain, along with considerable edema. They said it would be days before they knew what the outcome would be. An ultrasound also showed that she had a blocked renal artery, which had caused the high blood pressure.

I was feeling quite stressed and thought that I had better see about my own condition. I checked into the Primary Care Clinic at the hospital, where they gave me blood pressure medication and an anti-anxiety medication. It was then I found out that my left carotid artery was blocked. Thankfully, there was no need for immediate treatment, since the right carotid was open enough.

On the 22nd Jo's vital signs were looking better and she was moved to a step-down unit. By the end of the month Jo had shown considerable improvement. She was able to mouth some familiar words and was able to swallow. Jo was scheduled to move into rehab at Moultrie Creek Nursing and Rehabilitation Center on the 31st.

Jenifer flew to St. Augustine on the 30th. I was sure glad to see her, and glad that she'd been able to see her mother while she was still in the hospital. Jo was moved to rehab the next day. Jenifer took a lot of the moving burden upon herself. This was of immeasurable help. She assembled and labeled the clothing requested by Rita Magruder, the Moultrie Creek nurse responsible for Jo's care. Jenifer collected pictures to put in Jo's room, gathered Jo's boom box and a collection of CD's, collected personal items that would aid Jo's comfort, and bought a little stuffed white cat to take Lacey's place. Jenifer spent a lot of time with her mother during those first days at Moultrie Creek. She took care of her nails, helped feed her, and massaged her feet and hands.

Jenifer was also good company for me. She helped a lot with meals and keeping house, and best of all, kept me from being alone. Larry drove down on August 4th. Jenifer and Larry went home together on the 11th.

33 – The Healing Road

At Moultrie Creek, Jo started a regimen of speech therapy, occupational therapy to regain use of her right hand and arm, and physical therapy to regain use of her right leg and prevent muscle contractures. The first two weeks she showed marked progress. She was naming colors and speaking several words. During one of our visits I asked her if she wanted to hear some music. She said, "Yep!" I was so thrilled and thankful at that response, because it was a response she made without any prompting. A week later she was saying multi-syllable words in therapy and was talking with me afterwards.

We had a disheartening setback on the 23rd of August. Rita called me at five-thirty in the morning to tell me that Jo had been found on the floor beside her bed, and that she was being taken to the hospital. We really don't know what happened, except she had a pneumatic mattress that inflated on alternate sides periodically, to turn her in bed and help prevent bedsores. Perhaps it had raised her high enough on one side that she went over the bed rails. Fortunately, she had not experienced any serious injuries, but she had accumulated fluid in her lungs. After eight days she was sufficiently recovered to enable her return to Moultrie Creek.

Meanwhile, Jenifer had sent her mother a greeting card with a bobcat kitten on the front. When I gave it to Jo on the day of her return, she broke out crying deeply.

"Are you crying because you miss Lacey?"

She nodded, "Yes."

I got a soft-sided pet carrier and took Lacey in the next day. When I showed Lacey to Jo, she just beamed and hugged Lacey to her side. She held Lacey for quite a while, and Lacey was totally relaxed and snuggled up to her.

By the following day we were continuing to see more and more signs of improvement. Jo became much more alert, was sometimes in a playful mood, and sometimes quite coquettish, moving her shoulders in time to some background music from a TV. She was very interested in my new cell phone and didn't want to give it back to me. Surprisingly, she was less interested in having me play any music for her, and wanted me to talk. She said "nope" and "yep" to several questions, tried to talk about other things that came up in our conversation, and laughed appropriately at several things.

On my visit the next day I played a recording of one of the programs she had done at WNDA. She started lip-syncing the words to all of the songs, and seemed very surprised when she heard her own voice on the recording. This brought on a bit of nostalgia. We prayed and I started to get ready to go home. Then they brought her dinner. The CNA asked me if I was going to feed her. Jo's facial expressions told me she wanted me to feed her, so I did.

I got to Moultrie Creek at two o'clock on Labor Day, the 4th. Jo was awake, but appeared quite tired. I lowered her bed and she drifted off to sleep. When she awoke we had Communion. She was now trying very hard to talk. I told her, "I love you."

She replied, "I love you too."

Later, with a little prompting from Rita, she said, "Give me a kiss."

Communication sometimes became very difficult. Jo was more responsive to me and tried very hard to talk to me, but I was not always able to make out her words. She would become frustrated, and I hurt because she couldn't get through to me.

Two days passed. I was playing a CD for her, and all was well until they started Church in the Wildwood. Then it got better. Jo started singing along with the CD, and most of her words were audible. On my next visit, she was resting comfortably. We had a good visit and, surprisingly, she didn't want to hear any music, look at any books, or have me read to her. She just wanted to be with me. When I left at four-fifty she said loudly and clearly, "Goodnight, Dick."

Jo showed overall improvement the rest of September. The gain was not steady, however. Some days were good, other days were not so good. She was constantly battered by periods of depression and periods of pain. Usually any reminder of home would bring on sadness. This became quite clear when I asked her one Friday, "Would you like me to bring Lacey in tomorrow?" and she said, "No." Nor did she want me to bring Lacey in anymore.

She had a lot of pain, most of it from the strains of physical therapy. "Help me to stop ---. Help me to stop hurting." The overall improvement was encouraging, though. Instead of lip-syncing the words to hymns, she sang the words out loud.

One day I took her a bouquet of flowers. Her face lit up when she saw them. She reached for and took them with her right hand. I asked her, "Who brought you the flowers?"

She replied, with a coy smile, "My boyfriend."

She did not want to listen to poetry or music, she just wanted to be quiet with me and hold hands. For the first time, she was not using a tight grip with her right hand, and was using the arm and hand quite a bit. "Your right hand is getting better."

She said, "Yes."

By the end of the month the physical therapist was starting to teach Jo how to use a wheelchair. Everything was going fine until we got out in the hall. Then Jo started crying deeply. I sensed that she, seeing other folks in wheelchairs, thought this was going to be her life. Talking things out with her showed this was the case. I tried to convince her that the wheelchair was just a step toward walking again. That day brought several sessions of deep crying, some due to her realizing how much her life had changed, some due to a feeling that she wasn't getting better. I tried to persuade her that she was getting better, and the fact that they were moving her along was proof.

By October, Jo was much better. She slept less and we were able to do more. There were many things we did together and our life seemed to have acquired a rhythm. I gave her Communion several times. She was eating by herself, with a little help from the staff and me. I read to her frequently – the Bible, poetry, and we read the funnies together. Jenifer called her frequently. Jo enjoyed getting the phone calls, even though she was limited to listening and making simple responses.

We did exercises recommended by the different therapists, and, of course, we listened to gospel music CD's and watched gospel DVD's. Every once in a while Jo would start crying, especially during a favourite hymn. She nodded assent when I asked her if the hymns reminded her of the life she once enjoyed. It was obvious she was grieving over the life she no longer had. There were recurring periods of grief, which I think was understandable and to be expected. Overall, Jo's morale was good, and the staff reported that she seemed to be trying, and was making progress. I noticed she seemed to be increasingly taking more charge of her life. I was really surprised one day when one of the aides ran up to her and said, "I am so proud of you. I saw you taking those steps." She hugged Jo and kissed her on the cheek. By month's end Jo was noticeably stronger, and was telling us more about what she wanted, rather than nodding or shaking her head in response to questions. Our activities now included visits to the facility's ice cream parlor and wheelchair walks around the grounds.

November was a time of perceptible progress, despite Jo having a bout with stomach flu and occasional periods of introspection. Jo did not sleep as much during our visits as she had before. We talked, watched DVD's, listened to CD's, I read to her, we took long wheelchair walks outside, had phone conversations with Jenifer, and worked on some of her therapy exercises. Jo was able to communicate her wants to me through words I could understand. Especially gratifying was her desire to take Communion.

Jo's Medicare benefits came to an end on November 13th. I had a conference with the social worker, head therapist, and the unit's head nurse to determine a Post-Medicare care plan. We discussed Jo's progress so far, where progress could be improved, current goals, and what the care plan would be. Stressed was the possibility and desire to get her ready for discharge, possibly by year's end.

I saw Jo before the conference. She was in her wheelchair, looked good, and was listening to a CD. After the conference, she was in bed, but awake. We talked about the conference and the possibility of her being able to go home. I recognized that she did not think she was getting any better, and we worked on that for a while. But she did perk up when a therapist came in the room and said, "I hear that they are going to do a home evaluation for you. That is great."

As the days moved on, Jo became more mobile and was attending social functions in the facility. I caught her coming from a Bingo game one day, and I attended a birthday party with her. At that party we sat with four other women and one of their sons. All of the women were older than Jo, and two of them were former stroke patients who had recovered from disabilities similar to Jo's. This greatly encouraged Jo.

For Thanksgiving, Jenifer and Larry sent a bouquet of yellow mums, one of Jo's favourite flowers. Larry had also made a DVD of pictures that he and Jenifer took on their recent trip to Atlanta, and Jenifer put together a CD of favourite songs that Jo did not have on other CD's. Jo enjoyed watching the pictures on our portable DVD player and listening to the CD.

On Wednesday, November 22nd I met Jo in the dining hall for a pre-Thanksgiving breakfast for residents and their families. Jo ate a very good breakfast (more than I did) and fared pretty well. Regretfully,

I had to leave at nine-twenty to keep an appointment at Flagler Hospital for a blood sugar test and tutoring on blood sugar control. I went back at three in the afternoon. Jo was in her room napping. After she woke up, we talked about the morning and what had happened at the hospital, we read the funnies, said our prayers, and listened to a CD. 'Twas a good visit.

 The next day Jo seemed to be in pretty good spirits. She did not want to do anything except be quiet and be together. We read the funnies and talked about the day's trivia. Jenifer and Larry called, and that excited Jo. She communicated to me that she wanted a clock, and we did a bit of talking to find out what kind she wanted. We said prayers. When I started the prayers, I said, "The Lord be with you."

 Jo replied, "And also with you."

 This was a most blessed first for us.

 On Friday afternoon, I found Jo in the ice cream parlor. I gave her a multicolored poinsettia, which pleased her greatly. We went to her room and I showed her the clock I had bought. She liked it. I asked her what time it was and she said, "Quarter after three," which was pretty close. She decided where she wanted it and I hung it on the wall for her.

 Weekends were times of rest and recovery from five days of rather intensive therapy. When I went to her room on Saturday, Jo was sleeping. She awoke with some stomach distress. I sat quietly with her until she felt better. We read the funnies and spent quite a bit of time talking about the day's events. There wasn't an aide handy when dinner came, so I helped her eat by cutting her food into bite-sized pieces. This pleased her greatly, and I was greatly encouraged by the progress that she was making.

 On Sunday, Jo was in her room resting. She was in pretty good spirits, and showed more control over her right hand. I read some of the Sunday funnies to her, and, to my surprise and pleasure, she took the paper from me, held it with both hands, and read two full pages herself. She did not want music, or me to read to her, so we just talked. Our neighbor, Kim, and her daughter, Elizabeth, came in, bringing Jo a red poinsettia and a little silver Christmas tree. Elizabeth hung some red garland over the draperies. Dinner came at five-fifteen, and I helped Jo with her food and stayed with her while she ate.

 Monday marked the beginning of another week of therapy. I met Jo in the ice cream parlor at two-thirty, where she was indulging in her favourite flavor, butter pecan. I noticed a knitted sleeve on her left arm.

That told me they had started teaching her to use her hand to propel her wheelchair, as well as her feet. Wonderful! Another positive step on the road to recovery. After she finished her ice cream, we went outside for a long walk and watched the staff put up Christmas decorations in the courtyard. We went back in at about four o'clock and Jo lay down for a rest. I gave her a manicure and cut her toenails. It was rough for this inexperienced male, but I got it done without hurting either one of us. We read the funnies, said our prayers, and by that time, dinner came. I helped Jo with her dinner and left at six o'clock.

    It was dark when I got home, and as I walked through the garage I just blurted out without thinking, "Lord, if you take Jo, take me also!" I caught myself up short; "Where did that come from?" After such a good time together I had no reason to suspect that anything was amiss.

34 – The End of Our World

The telephone rang at six in the morning on Tuesday, November 28, 2006. It was Rita from Moultrie Creek. "Richard?"

"Yes."

"This is Rita. Jo has just died. We coded her, but could not bring her around."

"I'll be right over."

"There is no rush. Be careful and take it easy. Would you like me to call Richard?"

"Yes, please do."

I threw the phone on the bed and cried out, "God, how could you do this to me?"

I called Larry and had him tell Jenifer. It was a hard and bitter blow for her. She and her mother could not have been closer. I dressed and left for Moultrie Creek for a last visit there with my bride.

Later, I talked with Jenifer and asked her how she felt about taking Jo back to Huntsville, where her parents and two of our boys are buried. Jenifer heartily approved. We were fortunate enough to get a double plot in Maple Hill Cemetery, the old downtown cemetery where Kenneth and Ian are buried. We had often walked in the cemetery after church on Sundays. It was a favourite place of ours. Jenifer and Larry, and Charles and Joan Grover came to Florida for her burial service.

We celebrated a Requiem Mass for Melba Josephine on December 1, at Church of the Reconciliation. Fr. Robert Marsh was the celebrant, Canon Burt Froehlich gave the eulogy, and Fr. David Wiedner of Trinity Parish assisted. Burt asked me for a significant comment on Jo's life. My reply was, **"She would not 'break a bruised reed nor quench a smoldering wick.'"** (*ref. Matthew 12:20,* RSV) Such was my experience with that very wise, gentle, loving, and patient lady.

Two days later we took Jo "home" to Huntsville, Alabama, and laid her to rest on December 4th.

Afterword

During the following months I kept as busy as possible to battle the loneliness. I became quite weary and on March 2nd took my first nap since Jo went into the hospital. After an hour and a half I woke up hearing an inner voice. "Your world died when Jo died." That shook me considerably, and after I had time to digest the words I realized that yes, the world as I knew it did die with Jo, and I would have to find what my world was now. I resolved to take just one day at a time and do whatever God put in front of me to do.

Jesus told his disciples, "In my Father's house, there are many mansions; if it were not so, I would have told you. I go to prepare a place for you." (*John 14:2, KJV*) I took these words to heart and my fervent prayer became, **"Lord Jesus, please prepare a place for me, and prepare me to be fit for that place. And, if possible, when my task here on earth is finished, let Jo meet me and guide me home."**

In the midst of all of my grief, I became painfully conscious of St. Paul's words, "In everything give thanks: for this is the will of God in Christ Jesus concerning you." (*1 Thessalonians 5:18, KJV*) How could I be thankful when I had lost so much? And then, I thought, "Yes. Thank you, God, for giving me Jo and for all the years we had together. Thank you, God, for showing me what love could be through our life together. Thank you, God, for the four months and eight days after the stroke when all we could do was be together and love each other. Thank you, God, that she is now free of pain and suffering, and thank you, God, that she is now at home with you and Jesus."

On July 20th, the fiftieth anniversary of our wedding, I wrote the following in my journal:

"Fifty- years ago today, God gave me Melba Josephine Golden to be my bride. I forever thank and bless him for the wonderful gift she is to me. I wish that we were together to celebrate the gift."

Even though we are physically separated, Jo is still with me on the journey, and Jesus gives me the will and strength to continue.

Poems by Jo

Melba Josephine Marshall

With comments by Richard G. Marshall

Table of Contents

The Picnic	147
untitled - 1981	149
Elsa's Song	150
Autumn Rainsong	151
September Tenth	153
Bluebird	154
untitled - Spring, 1991	155
Spring, 1991	156
The Lady Shirt	157
Companions	158
To Frances	159
untitled - September, 1991	161
untitled - 1995	162

The Picnic

You promised a picnic
but it rained that day,
but before my hopes
could give in to dismay
you said,
"We'll go anyway."

So umbrellas hoisted
we strode to the woods.
The creek was roaring
as though stop us it could
as we found a place
that to us seemed good.

We crossed on a log
that spanned the creek,
with legs that were trembling
and knees that were weak,
a sheltered place
from rain to seek.

We climbed the hill
emerging from mire,
our clothing caught
on many a briar,
our legs aching,
beginning to tire.

The old apple orchard
came into sight,
and the old wooden bench
where we thought we might
enjoy our repast
with much delight.

Boiled eggs, hot tomato soup
and fruit we ate
as our appetites
we sought to sate
before wearily climbing
the old wooden gate
to home.

> unknown
>
> *The description fits the area around Jo's home in Warren, Michigan; the picnic probably took place during the late 1940's.*

(untitled – 1981)

Go My Child - live, love, be free
Do not cling so much to me
I'm not turning you out in the cold
Live, live before you are old.

It is now too late for me
Somehow, I was never free
Go, go, My Child, be bold
Too soon, too old.

1981

Probably written to Jenifer at a time of transition in her life. I believe it was Jo giving Jenifer the freedom to "be." The poem could also be a reflection on the relationship Jo had with her mother.

Elsa's Song

You were there at my birthing, Oh Angel of Mercy.
You were there at my waking to joy
and to pain.
The unspeakable joy of all Love's completeness
Taken now from me.
Unspeakable pain!
Though space and time now separate us,
Wait not 'til my sleeping
to come yet again.

From Shades of Grey, 1983

Originally written as part of her novel, I found that this poem expressed my feelings twenty-three years later.

Autumn Rainsong

I really can't explain
why I love an autumn rain.
Others laugh at me
and my apparent glee,
as I shrug into a sweater
and face upturned I taste
the elixir of the heavens.

Others run and cower
when grey skies begin to glower,
but I truly find it bracing
when leaves and clouds are racing.
Water needles sting my face
(and with ice it's even better)
as I turn it for a taste of weather.

Not just a gentle natter,
a tiny pitter-patter,
but a slanting, driving sheet
that may turn into sleet.
Torrents from the heavens above,
cruel and cold. I really love
a wintry sky purpled much like heather.

When the wind is clean and cold
my blood becomes quite bold.
I find it to my liking
to think I was a Viking.
A Northern wind tossed sea
in my genetic memory is freedom,
and yet is never-never.

A longing for my past
comes in every wintry blast.
Who and what was I back then
when history was dim?
What sets my spirit free
is a mystery to me,
but it surely rides upon the autumn weather.

To soar upon the breeze
and go where e'er I please,
borne aloft by wind and rain
and then return again.
Not to see things as before
for through an open door
I have glimpsed the ever-ever.

Summer, 1990

Jo's favourite season was autumn. She used to love standing on a hill and letting the wind blow in her face.

September Tenth

I do not want to write of his death
until the sharp edges of pain
have blurred.
But I cannot stop myself thinking.
So, I'll remember:
the beautiful black butterfly
that hovered and flew above us
as we dug his grave;

That the magnolia bloomed
one perfect bloom,
'tho it was September,
Celebrating his Life
with beauty
amid the dead yellow leaves,
and not the sadness
of his leaving;

A small mound on the embankment,
under the dogwoods,
where red berries fell
in gentle tears,
as we marked his place
with a flat native stone
from
the woods.

September 10, 1991

The day we buried Thomas A-Beckett, the beloved black angora cat we had for eight years.

Bluebird

A flash of blue across my grey morning,
Lighting wintry-bare dogwood's branch.
"Too soon," I cry inside.
"Spring is too distant."
Yet, there again he flies,
Slicing through my January heart, with beauty.
And,
Again he comes, thrice in all,
Penetrating my dullness.
Waking me to see dark green spears
Peering through brown leaves,
Into an uncertain world of cold,
With hope of a soon coming sun,
Warming them to yellow.

January 29, 1991

(untitled – Spring, 1991)

How still you lie, the waters caressing you,
Spreading your feathery tresses about
your motionless form.

Sleep, endless sleep has encompassed you.
No more the whirring of wings
Nor mournful sigh.

But wait. . .

Slowly I approach in somber reverence.
You stir!
Startled, we stare eye to eye.

Then shaking off the watery shroud,
You rise again
To the sky.

Leaving me amid droplets
As of rain,
But glad!

Spring, 1991

"This actually happened. It was a dove sleeping in the birdbath."
(Jo)

Spring, 1991

Today I gathered flowers
to bring the outside in.

White with pink, yellow or orange.
Fourteen different, yet the same.

Their frail beauty pressed hard against my hand
by the rising wind.

Promised showers rode
the low grey clouds.

Defeated, the pale sun withdrew
its warmth giving way to chill.

Climbing the hill, head bent before the quickening weather
I inhaled the sweetness of blooms.

Gaining the house, I placed the scented captives
in crystal vases.

The rain racing down the panes could not reach.

1991

The Lady Shirt

My daughter brought it back to me,
saying,
"I think one of us should preserve this."
Smiling,
she handed me the old shirt.

Thin, pale green,
with lovely art nouveau
ladies in lavender,
it lay limply in my hand.
"Ah, yes, we must, for it is so much more
than it seems."
Happy memories flooded
our beings.

We each had several of
the many coloured "Lady Shirts,"
Mom, Jenny and me.
And laughing, we seemed to float
through soft summer evenings,
as we wore them
where we most wanted
to be.

Caressing the remnant of those hours,
I held its softness to my cheek.
Dancing around the room
we heard again the music
that spoke to our souls.
Laughing giddily, dizzily,
we collapsed on the bed
and wept.

Summer, 1990

Companions

Together they sat, plying their needles,
    Each engrossed in her own task and thoughts.
One drove the steel through thick layers,
    Crafting warmth for long winter nights.
Delicate tracks crossing fields of printed flowers
    blooming endlessly day and night,
To cover young lovers or
        older dreamers.

The other's steel pierced canvas,
    Bringing to life more flowers to bloom and
Cushion weary bodies at day's end.
    Woolen roses and leaf bright greens
Intertwining
        softness and warmth.

September, 1991

Gran was sewing one of her quilts and Jo was doing a needlepoint picture.

To Frances

Sometimes I miss you.
On days like today,
I miss you
Coming in cold, asking for a fire.
I miss the smile in your blue eyes
As I comply with your request and give you what you desire.
Sometimes I miss you.

Sometimes I miss you
As sunlight warms the land.
I miss you
Strolling down the path, inspecting the garden,
Helping plant tiny seeds, pressing me to stop
And sit with you (as you proceed with your bath).
Sometimes I miss you.

Sometimes I miss you
Alone at afternoon tea.
I miss you –
The warmth of your nearness – inquisitiveness, interest,
Especially alert at the beating of eggs,
Your favourite dish.
I still turn to see if you are there on your chair.
Sometimes I miss you.

Sometimes I miss you
When startled by a picture of someone
Very like you.
I miss you.
Companionship, aggravation, delight
Eighteen years, now gone.
Others have come and gone
But still
Sometimes I miss you.

1991

Frances was our part Siamese daughter of Phyllis. She was eighteen years old when she died. She had been my constant homework companion while we were in Texas.

(untitled – September, 1991)

Sometimes I am my Mother
Sometimes I am my Child
Sometimes I am neither
but myself alone.
And yet
No one is ever himself alone.

Sometimes my Mother is her Mother
Sometimes my Mother is me
Sometimes she is my Child
Sometimes she is none
but herself alone.

Sometimes my Child is me
Sometimes she is my Child
Sometimes she is my Mother
Sometimes she is none
but herself alone.

Sometimes we are one
Sometimes we are none
Sometimes we are ourselves alone.
Unique. . . and yet,
No one is ever himself alone.

(After meeting my Mother
in a dimly lit hall,
in the wee hours,
She looked like us all.)

September, 1991

*Written shortly after we moved
back to Huntsville.*

(untitled – 1995)

Momma said she would always be there.
Her fierce love could break every snare.
No one could ever show more care.

She sits now with vacant stare.
Greets us with wrong names –
Unaware.
There, but not there.

Tears run down her sad wrinkled face.
As she too seeks a momma
No longer there.

1995

*After one of our visits to Gran at
Alice Kidd Nursing Home.*

www.ingramcontent.com/pod-product-compliance
Ingram Content Group UK Ltd.
Pitfield, Milton Keynes, MK11 3LW, UK
UKHW041011220326
11408UKWH00001B/116